THE BLACKSMITH AND THE FARMER

The Blacksmith and the Farmer

Rural Manufacturing in sub-Saharan Africa

DAVID POSTON

INTERMEDIATE TECHNOLOGY PUBLICATIONS
1994

Intermediate Technology Publications
103/105 Southampton Row, London WC1B 4HH, UK

© David Poston 1994

ISBN 1 85339 127 1

Typeset by Dorwyn Ltd, Rowlands Castle, Hants
Printed in Great Britain by BPC Wheatons Ltd, Exeter

Contents

Preface

THE MANIE BLACKSMITHS' cry for tools with which to work resulted in five weeks spent making tools with them in 1987. The very positive results of this second visit and the realization that the blacksmiths are able to develop themselves and their colleagues led to a third visit in 1988, at the blacksmiths' request.

It is sadly typical of working for development that the initial success of these visits led the author to be invited to join ITDG to do work which precluded further visits to Manie. In spite of some interest, the agricultural centre at Lusekele has been unable to raise the necessary funds for the indigenous training system in whose inception the Manie blacksmiths played such a major part. The skills introduced to the smiths have been maintained, and some training of other smiths continued for a period, though subsequently there has been no means of monitoring this.

However, the initial lessons learned in Manie continued to be exploited within the ITDG Rural Workshops Programme in projects in Malawi, Zimbabwe and, most recently, Tanzania and have been corroborated by the experiences which other programme staff brought from elsewhere. The results of the experience of the ITDG team have been incorporated in this book. Particularly relevant to the lessons indicated by the author has been the work of Godfrey Cromwell, Dave Harries, Bernhard Heer, Brighton Melani, Joseph Marihwi, Aaron Moore, Andy Rowe and Andrew Scott. A textbook for blacksmithing instructors and a manual for African rural blacksmiths by Dave Harries, and Harries and Heer respectively are also being published by IT Publications in order to convey particular practical lessons learned from the process. ITDG and its various local partners are continuing to develop, adapt and spread the system as they continue to learn from the artisans.

It is not the intention of the author to suggest that artisanal development is the only area of manufacturing which can contribute to the rural development process, but rather to draw attention to its vital contribution and to indicate that it is possible to arrive at an appropriate methodology.

Although this book particularly describes work with traditional blacksmiths it is hoped that the relevance of the methodology which it proposes as a contribution to the consolidation and development of other rural skills will also be recognized and exploited.

This book is an amended version of the author's PhD thesis for the University of Warwick, submitted in 1991. His initial recognition of the significance of traditional blacksmithing to rural economies came during a study visit to Zaire and Zambia in 1986.

Acknowledgements

I wish to acknowledge the help and support of all those who have taught me, particularly Dr Terry Thomas and the Development Technology Unit, Warwick University, the Intermediate Technology Development Group (ITDG), the School of Art of the University of Humberside, Gary Selig and, above all, the blacksmiths of Manie and my wife, Frances.

Introduction

THERE IS CONSIDERABLE potential for the development of rural manufacturing in central Africa, but it lies within the existing structures of practice rather than in the introduction of Northern systems and practices, which normally involve radical change and the inappropriate use of capital.

The fundamental purpose of consolidating and developing rural manufacturing is the support of agriculture and the agricultural community. Metalworking has been focused upon in this study because in this context the role of rural blacksmiths in providing capital equipment for local agriculture and income-generating activities is vital, particularly in poorer economies. Contrary to popular opinion, traditional blacksmithing is still common in central Africa and constitutes an important resource for rural development and industrialization.

The popularly assumed dominance of imports and large-scale manufacturing is undermined by the lack of foreign exchange, standardized production inappropriate to local conditions, distribution difficulties and the need for repairs which can be carried out locally. The contribution of the two systems for the production of metal goods to rural income generation and development is also compared. Rural industrialization is shown to be the most beneficial.

Examining the viability of rural manufacturing, the existing structures of rural manufacturing practice reflect the prevailing conditions under which production takes place and therefore contain features which are fundamentally appropriate to their context. An approach to intervention is therefore proposed which capitalizes on existing skills, practices and social relationships rather than requiring the development of new practitioners, skills and social relationships, and it is shown that by working with existing structures and skills rather than undermining them, the sustainability of the enterprises which are developed is greatly enhanced.

Most traditional blacksmithing is carried out by farmers who are part-time smiths, some of whom are more active than others. As part of the communities they serve, they take advantage of scrap material, respond to local conditions and preferences and conserve resources by their important repair activities. Money spent on their products remains within the community. The evidence shows that external agents concerned with rural industrialization generally dismiss the significance of the activity because it is part-time and has a very low profile, and instead attempt to create full-time enterprises which are unlikely to be viable in rural areasand which ignore existing cultural patterns. Northern entrepreneurial attitudes and an assumption that rural communities are fully integrated with the cash economy further decrease the penetration and sustainability of external efforts.

An important proposition is that the extent of the problems involved in rural development in Africa makes it essential that developments in rural activities are able to spread of their own accord, being adopted and adapted by the people without any further external assistance. Unless an intervention is designed in all aspects from the beginning for the results to be free-standing and appropriate for autonomous propagation, the effort, in comparison to the cost and the scale of the problem, will be wasted. Duplication is frequently referred to as the desirable end, but any duplication which requires the support of an external agent in order to occur each time is unrealistic in terms of improving the situation of the rural population on a significant scale.

Autonomous propagation can only occur if the development takes advantage of the existing resources of rural people and is of a sufficiently small order of magnitude that it constitutes an acceptable level of risk in their economically marginal situation. Such change should be incremental, and needs to involve a cost low enough to make it widely accessible and viable, at the same time as making sufficient difference to justify the effort. If an intervention seeks to create an activity which requires a substantially new set of skills the development is unlikely to propagate autonomously since it is unlikely to find existing fertile ground in which to grow and is therefore an excessive risk.

Having demonstrated that an opportunity exists for the development of sustainable rural industrialization which can spread, this book examines in detail the existing practices of intervention agents and proposes an alternative strategy, showing examples of its success. The principles of the methodology are described below.

In order to work with existing human resources external agents must recognize their value and understand the nature of existing capability. Technical interventions should not contain an assumed technological goal but, starting from existing resources, should be concerned with finding the most accessible way to meet the given need. Using the status quo as the departure point for interventions minimizes the distorting assumptions and external values which the agent will bring to the problem and the degree of change to which the participants will be subjected. Since considerable change is inevitable, unnecessary change should be avoided. Agents must respect indigenous knowledge and the appropriateness of it in context.

Even where an enterprise has received external support to develop, there invariably comes a time when it is left to its own devices. Since the environment within which rural enterprises exist in Africa is changing rapidly the ability of the enterprise to change and adapt in relation to circumstances is essential to its survival. Rural artisans therefore need to be flexible problem solvers, rather than information-based workers. Design and Analytical Decision Making can play a significant part in the activities of a small workshop and make an essential contribution to its development.

Adaptation and innovation involve experimentation and risk, for which self-confidence is essential. This book examines how the respect with which practitioners are regarded by themselves, their community and any external agents with whom they are working significantly affects their confidence. Thus, again, external agents must respect existing practices and what has been achieved with minimal resources in order to develop the confidence of those whom they seek to assist, rather than impatiently promote the superiority of their Northern knowledge.

Northern formal education systems are prevalent in Africa, and have goals and produce results appropriate to the requirements of Northern industrial and post-industrial societies. Northern education systems condition graduates to Northern values and systems and therefore affect the attitudes of external agents whether they are Northern or

African. Since Northern vocational training systems are designed to provide workers for large-scale modern industry they are inappropriate to the needs of existing or would-be rural practitioners. Small-scale rural manufacturing in Africa is essentially pre-industrial; training for it which forms part of an intervention must recognize this and should be undertaken in an environment which resembles that of subsequent practice as closely as possible. Established training workshops in institutions bear minimal resemblance to the environment in which rural artisans will work, and should therefore not be used. Training systems which develop the local sharing of knowledge and which relate to the traditional apprenticeship system are more appropriate and contribute to a community's ability to train and develop itself.

The target-orientation of most Northern-conditioned external agents and development interventions is examined, and it is shown that it results in a tendency to be concerned with the achievement of short-term goals at the expense of incremental development which can be sustained and which can subsequently propagate itself unassisted. The repeated failure of development interventions which succumb to the introduction of unsustainable elements, often minor, is used to demonstrate that actions prompted by short-term expediency result in long-term failure.

The human resources necessary for the development of rural manufacturing already exist widely in Africa but a failure to recognize them has led to attempts to re-create them in ways inappropriate to the production of sustainable results. It is not the resources which are lacking, but an understanding of the ways in which they can be fruitfully supported and developed.

1. Rural Industrialization

Identifying a strategy for small-scale rural industrialization

STRATEGIES FOR RURAL industrialization must take into consideration a wide range of factors. The delicacy of the rural economic social and environmental ecology demands that careful attention be given to the complete context, however apparently insignificant certain aspects of it may appear. The identification and analysis of relevant factors by outsiders with a perspective far removed from the empirical understanding of the village people concerned is fraught with risk to the subjects and to the developmental goal. Minimizing such risk must be a primary concern; to do so requires the maximum possible respect for existing local skills, knowledge and perceptions. The principle of working outwards from the rural *status quo* is fundamental, since working inwards constitutes the imposition of alien assumptions, with the inevitable concomitant unforeseen negative effects.

If rural industrialization is to be affected from within it is essential that the base from which it is to be developed is understood well, since this indicates the direction, speed and manner of development which are practicable. An examination of existing technical skills and perceptions and the manner in which these are acquired and transmitted is necessary, in order that the means to augment them and improve their communication may be identified. In considering the development of the means of transmission of technical knowledge, the introduction of contributions by external agents should at all times be minimized, since any system of technical extension dependent upon external action is limited in its scope and potential. This is not to deny the value of well-focused appropriate external contributions at particular points in time, but the development of effective actions originating internally must always be the priority. 'Ascending technical development', (bottom-up), can only succeed if propagation becomes autonomous, the generation of impetus and the growth of capability being brought about by the action of the rural industrialists, the artisans, themselves. Since successful propagation is fundamental to extensive rural industrialization, an understanding of existing structures and capabilities is necessary, in order that these may be capitalized upon and adapted and developed to meet the needs of the proposed expansion of the artisans' activities.

For autonomous propagation to be possible, the essential knowledge must be owned by the artisans involved. Since additional technical knowledge is necessary for development, the volume of it, in particular the quantitative ratio of new and old knowledge, and the manner in which the new is introduced are highly significant. A massive introduction of technical knowledge devalues inherited wisdom and the value of ownership of it, while the imposition of alien structures denies the value of the existing social patterns. For this reason the purpose of any external input must be clearly defined, the input occurring only when existing alternatives are manifestly inadequate for the required development. Existing technology and structure need to be examined regarding their adequacy in relation to each other and the purposes for which they are required, in order that changes will only be introduced where they are most urgently required. The recognition and rejection of gratuitous improvements, conforming to the perceptions of outsiders, is necessary if the existing base is to be consolidated rather than wasted.

In identifying the factors which inhibit rural industrialization, in order to propose the means of amelioration, the significance of infrastructure and the desirability and manner of its development must be considered. Muller contends that infrastructure is the single most crucial factor restraining rural industrialization, but also argues that the real need is for the development of an infrastructure suitable to subsistence agriculture which will, incidentally, serve the needs of artisans (blacksmiths, in the case of his study). He postulates further that rural industry, in the case of blacksmithing, is sufficiently developed to meet the needs of subsistence agriculture as it is currently practised (Muller 1980). While infrastructural restraints are highly significant their removal is not the panacea which Muller suggests. The extent of the restraint and the degree to which it needs to be addressed must therefore be examined.

2

If development is to be appropriate to its context, and is to be primarily effected by existing practitioners, the ability to develop and adapt apposite techniques and structures is necessary. In order to establish the potential for rural industrialization it is necessary to examine the extent of the indigenous ability to design and innovate, and the relationship between innovation and the society in which it occurs. If significant contemporary innovative capability is not in evidence the possibility and suitability of the introduction of relevant assistance from external sources needs to be examined, as does the premise that local design skills are necessarily the most appropriate.

While considerable work has been done regarding industrialization strategies, some of it according significance to the informal sector, the paucity of recorded data regarding indigenous small rural industries and the lack of formal structures make strategic generalizations difficult to prove. In order to identify a strategy for small-scale rural industrialization using indigenous structures the approach to this research has been largely empirical, particularly involving work with the blacksmiths of the village of Manie in Bandundu, Zaire. Where village industry has been considered in the past the emphasis has generally been on the establishment of new artisans, products of Northern-style technical training and thus primarily urban-oriented. While this approach has some relevance, it depends primarily upon the assumption that there are few traditional craftsmen remaining (Muller 1980:6), and a failure to perceive their relevance where they do still exist. In many areas there remain traditional artisans who constitute the most viable potential basis for rural industrialization (see next section); one of the principal barriers to their exploitation is ignorance of their significance on the part of urban-oriented outsiders, which is exacerbated by the considerable difficulties involved in working with such dispersed and informal groups.

The blacksmiths of Manie, Zaire

The survival of considerable indigenous blacksmithing activity in Africa to this day is somewhat surprising, considering the suppression to which it was frequently subjected under colonial rule and by missionaries resisting the fetishistic aspect of the activity. Besides direct suppression

3

for colonial economic or religious reasons, rural black-smithing had become an increasingly marginal activity due to the cost and quality advantages of centralized production, particularly when the location of production was in the technologically advanced countries which had long since experienced the industrial revolution. Prior to colonial occupation the ability to work iron had been one of the key factors permitting the territorial expansion of the Bantu people, the domination of particular tribes depending to a considerable extent upon their productive capability.

However, the domination of the market by centralized production is particularly dependent upon ease of transport and the availability of large quantities of new raw material to the industrial producers. Under colonial rule marketing and raw material collection were maintained as factors contributing to the commercial exploitation of the possessions in question. With the advent of independence many African countries were left short of both management and capital; in spite of some extension, transport and communications are now frequently seriously deficient and correspondingly expensive, making distribution from central manufacturers difficult, while population growth and the need for general rural development as opposed to limited cash-crop exploitation increase the pressure upon the system. The acute shortage of foreign exchange limits considerably the availability of new raw material stock to industrial manufacturers, as well as restricting the equipment available and frequently denying access to necessary spare parts for machinery fabricated abroad. The results are that industrial units often lack raw material in sufficient quantity to maintain production, that the shortage of efficient production plant necessitates increasingly artisan-based production, and that distribution becomes expensive, if not impossible. In addition, where an item was formerly imported and was not manufactured domestically, the shortage of foreign exchange restricts further imports or the setting up of mechanized production units, resulting in the limited availability of the product.

Since the bind in which most developing countries find themselves is largely the result of a colonialist economic structure, where low-priced raw material and agricultural exports pay for high-priced industrially processed imports, there is increasingly a move away from the conventional

4

import-export based economies to more self-contained and less dependent structures.

In this context the small rural workshop is rapidly becoming potentially less marginal. While there are still many problems, it is located among its clients, it requires a minimum of capital or technically complicated equipment and virtually no foreign exchange. In addition, in the case of blacksmiths, it is not necessary for the raw material to be standardized or new, which allows most available scrap to be exploited in one way or another; while there is frequently a shortage of scrap metal in rural areas its lower cost offsets the time required to collect it. Although the technical skills of the rural smiths may be limited, manual crafts have the virtue of being a most flexible form of manufacture, able to adjust to local and individual preference from item to item. The majority of rural blacksmithing is undertaken by those who, with their families, are also involved in subsistence agriculture and therefore benefit from the resilience of a mixed economy, even in extreme poverty. It is arguable that with some local infrastructural development and technical information input the activities of rural artisans could in the near future become pivotal once again.

Since the current practice of indigenous blacksmithing is largely the survivor of over a century of decline and repression, it is hardly surprising that the repertoire and skills of the smiths have suffered. In many cases the smithing knowledge will have been filtered through one person, as in the case of Waka Ngai of Manie, in Zaire, who has taught all the smiths of the village, directly or indirectly. This means that anything which he has mislearned or forgotten has become perverted or omitted from the tradition inherited by this particular group of smiths and all whom subsequently they train.

Particularly under colonial adminstration, but continuing since independence, the majority of African primary and secondary education is acquired almost entirely by rote learning, whose principal virtue is one of economy and simple duplication. The discouragement of analytical thought and problem-solving inherent in this system is exacerbated within most African rural societies by a prejudice against the advancement or initiative of the individual, which is perceived as divisive.

5

Many of the young people attending schools in rural areas of developing countries have come from a background of strong patriarchal discipline. Tribal chieftainship still exists and its authority is still great; probably their country has just emerged from colonialism. Under these regimes, initiative, responsibility and organising ability are not encouraged. But these qualities are vital in developing countries. (*Van Rensburg* 1974)

If the practice of rural blacksmithing had continued to be client-led and to evolve, the losses of technical knowledge over the last century would either not have occurred or could have been rapidly made good by innovation or re-invention. However, in the absence of significant analysis and innovation as normal practice the craft has depended almost entirely upon received knowledge, with inevitable diminution both through the failure to pass on information and with techniques such as smelting becoming obsolete.

During the original iron-age of the Bantu the craft would undoubtedly have been dynamic, developing through invention and the energetic acquisition of knowledge. In the long period of decline this ceased to be the case, with an increasingly limited production repertoire tailored to diminishing local activities; warfare and hunting are now largely not practised, so only agricultural and domestic needs remain. The *status quo* in Manie is a product list of three principal items: hoes, machetes and shovels, and a probable inability to re-develop the skills unassisted. The changed circumstances of rural Africa makes the resurgence of smithing, however, a most desirable, if not an essential factor; if this is to be achieved it is necessary for the craft to regain its former dynamism. Major external inputs may produce some manufacturing capacity, but it is likely to be urban based or lost to urban centres, and will not form an extension of existing social structures. Village smiths require raw materials, technical information, and developing markets; while modest external assistance in these matters is desirable, a general resurgence can only come about through the autonomous propagation of solutions by the smiths themselves. Large-scale comparatively capital-intensive attempts to develop this sector by external agencies will result inevitably in domination and in damage to a weak but functional part of the rural infrastructure. Growth, even if it is accelerated, must be organic if it is to be sustained; imposed artificial growth lacks the integrity to establish itself.

6

If some external assistance is to be given to rural black-smiths the approach taken is of paramount importance. Whatever shortcomings the knowledge and technology of the smiths may contain, a fundamental respect for their traditions, and for their capability and achievements within their context, is essential. Even where it may be considered that their traditions are of little cultural significance as a result of the evolution of their society over the last century, it is important to recognize that they continue to see themselves as the inheritors of a tradition and of the ancient skills contained within it. To disregard their place as masters of their craft is to patronize and denigrate them, the result of which would be to undermine their technical confidence and to encourage the rejection of existing practices and inherited capabilities. The continuing self-respect of the indigenous smiths in the face of industrially produced competition is essential if their existing knowledge and place within the community are to be capitalized upon for the purposes of rural development and their own well-being. It is significant that my contribution to the smiths at Manie was explained by their perception of me as a fond ancestor returned from the dead to help them; this rationale allowed my knowledge to become a part of their tradition, rather than remain an imposition from the white world and a suggestion of the inferiority of their knowledge.

If wisdom is seen as something precious, whose theft represents a serious threat, this wisdom must be treated with great respect and courtesy, however inadequate it may appear to Western eyes. To dismiss it is to dismiss its possessors; to fail to acknowledge its importance is to fail to acknowledge theirs. Failure in this fundamental outlook perpetuates the patronizing attitude of the white man, preventing communication and the engagement of indigenous artisans in their own development. The standardized imposition of Northern technology creates a demoralizing comparison with the indigenous knowledge of a traditional master, whose consequent failure to respond then perplexes and frustrates the unperceptive technology evangelist.

There is a considerable limitation on the amount that most people can learn in a given period of time, and the speed at which their knowledge can be advanced, since learning is contingent upon contributory knowledge having been previously assimilated. It is important, therefore, to restrict any input to the essential, excluding the merely desirable, in order to make it as beneficial as possible. In the case of Manie the input was restricted deliberately to the needs which the smiths themselves perceived and prioritized; they are the best judges of their own requirements, and things which they perceive are, by definition, close enough to their existing knowledge to be capable of assimilation.

> Respect for the poor and what they want offsets paternalism. The reversal this implies is that outsiders should start not with their own priorities but with those of the poor, although however much self-insight they have, outsiders will still project their own values and priorities. (Chambers 1983)

The pace of change is a key factor in maintaining the self-respect arising out of the possession of previously acquired knowledge. Where an excessive number of changes is made at one time the stability of the structure will be threatened, if the extent of the new knowledge diminishes and eclipses the old; the tradition will be denigrated in the eyes of its inheritors. For example, no changes were suggested to the form of bellows in use at Manie; although they are valveless and probably less than half as efficient as other appropriate types, they are sufficient to meet current requirements. Their improvement can wait until a later stage, when more urgent knowledge has been assimilated into the tradition. Although there is concern on the part of the outsider that the smiths in question will only receive one visit, resulting in the urge to give all the relevant knowledge possible at one time, this is likely to be counter-productive, and lead to minimal actual transfer. The technique of fire-welding was known by the smiths to exist as part of their tradition, but had not been retained within the Manie knowledge. Since it appeared possible that, with encouragement, they could acquire the technique from a member of their own tribe I deliberately did not demonstrate it, with their agreement. In their tradition fire-welding has associated laws and conventions which would be lost if it were to be re-introduced by a white outsider; we agreed that the maintenance of such customs was worth the risk of them failing to regain mastery of this important technique. (In the event the technique was demonstrated to several of the Manie smiths by a smith of the same tribe at the neighbouring village of Bangongo, on my last day with them.)

8

The key factor permitting a considerable amount of ground to be covered at Manie was that the majority of those involved are masters, very capable within their existing knowledge and used to working hard within a production context. While the period of time involved may appear unduly short it was in fact appropriate since they absorbed the additions to their knowledge easily, meantime being diverted from their essential income-generating production. The main delays were the length of time it takes to make an object, particularly for the first time, and the repetition by several people which forms the best route to the retention of the knowledge concerned. It would be unrealistic and over-optimistic to anticipate the retention of much more than 50 per cent of the input, in spite of the notes which were taken. I would expect the smiths to continue to be able to make nails, rivets, tongs, pincers and hammers, but suspect that the intricacies of heat treatment will soon become confused, preventing the competent making of edge tools such as pruning shears.

I did find an appropriate French-language functional (non-decorative) blacksmithing instructional book and copied the pages relevant to the techniques which we covered together, and sent them to Manie. While a complete instructional book could be sent it would be potentially intimidating, displaying a vast body of knowledge of which they are ignorant. The complete provision of such a book would be advisable only at a later stage, several input steps further on. One problem was that I was unable to find an instructional book on forgework which describes and works within the context of an indigenous African forge. Even where an African context has been used the accent is on a radical change of the working environment, in particular the raising of the working height from floor to waist, primarily to allow the introduction of Western-style equipment such as bellows, albeit Appropriate Technology (AT) versions. If indigenous forges in Africa are to be developed according to the principle of small acceptable stages it is essential that appropriate instructional material concerned with the step-by-step development of the forge from its current state is prepared. The total abandonment of the *status quo* in favour of a variation of the Western system is unrealistic in terms of the scale of the technological change involved, the demeaning of current practice and the comparatively high level of capital it would

9

require. In the context of Manie the introduction of one or other of the available designs for oil-drum bellows and forges would increase the capital required to establish a forge by as much as four times. If capital is a major restriction, as it is universally for the indigenous smith, the introduction of technical information full of inaccessible goodies will lead to considerable frustrations. That in this case the goodies can be home-built does not lessen the fact that the (scrap) raw materials alone represent an impossible investment. While much AT workshop equipment is highly suitable for a modern urban-style workshop, appropriateness relates directly to context, which in the case of the indigenous rural smith is very particular and also requires catering for. The publication of Aaron Moore's book *How to Make 12 Woodworking Tools* (IT Publications 1987) is an encouraging example of work that is appropriate to the most basic level of workshop. (It is significant that Moore's book arose out of his work as a VSO — Voluntary Service Overseas — volunteer, which was concerned with the most fundamental problems of technical development.) The need for a similar book for blacksmiths has since been met by *Basic Blacksmithing: an introduction to toolmaking* (IT Publications 1993), which Dave Harries and Bernhard Heer based upon their experience with ITDG in Africa.

The interest and involvement of Thomas Ngangu from Kilusu, together with the interest of Makoka Gimbungu, illustrate the eagerness of some rural artisans to gain access to technical assistance. Though I had little opportunity to meet other craftsmen on this visit, the workshops and individuals I met in Zaire and Zambia at the end of 1986 consistently persuaded me of the receptivity of the majority. Although this indicates a need for a system of technical assistance, in order for it to succeed, the approach, context and contents must be appropriate. The most direct route to this would be the development or introduction of an indigenous extension system, particularly if this would eventually lead to autonomous propagation. A major barrier is the habitual protection of wisdom, which makes the concept of the profitability of sharing as important to introduce as any set of techniques. In the case of the Manie smiths the experience of the benefits of shared knowledge, together with the possibility of a potential income from extending it to others and the reception of further knowledge as a conse-

10

quence of doing so appeared to be sufficient to persuade them that this change in their own attitudes is desirable. While there are undoubtedly risks and problems in attempting to initiate a scheme of indigenous technical centres, particularly in terms of exploitation, dominance, rivalry and misinformation, the immediate virtues and potential rewards of the approach would appear to justify the risk of its failure. If it succeeds it could enable the autonomous spread of shared information beyond the extent conceivably possible by a conventional extension centre.

The Western romantic notion that all practitioners of old crafts such as blacksmithing are automatically skilled is frequently applied to indigenous artisans in Africa. In many cases, including Manie, this is not the case. While capable within their context the extreme limitations of that context restrict to a great extent the degree to which they may be regarded as skilled. It is possible that this low level of artisanal skill has led many people to dismiss it altogether, regarding the remains of traditional iron-working as so degraded as to be of no value, leading to an attempt to generate a new set of artisans from scratch who subsequently exist in parallel with the remaining smiths of the indigenous tradition. However, unless major infrastructural change takes place, such as relocation to an urban environment, the limiting factors which affect the traditional rural smith will rapidly have their effect on the new craftsman. To suggest a limitation in indigenous skills is not to dismiss the potential that their possessors represent, but rather to comment on the context to which those skills refer. In the basic subsistence environment of many African villages the level of smithing that exists is largely appropriate to both agricultural technology and consumer resources, but if agriculture and incomes are to be developed, so must artisanal skills.

> Rural development implies increased agricultural production, but development means continually increasing production and continually increasing diversification of goods and services in both agriculture and industry. Development also implies that there should be a vigorous internal exchange of goods and services within the rural areas; production must not be limited only to exports abroad and exports to the modern sector but should be directed towards internal consumption as well. (Van Rensburg 1974)

11

Technical manufacturing skills cannot directly promote the development of agriculture, but if peasant agriculture is to be successfully developed an availability of adequate ancillary skills constitutes an essential factor. The indigenous smiths are already *in situ*, a part of the agricultural and social infrastructure, and are the most appropriate and economic means of making agricultural and domestic hardware available, and as such should be regarded seriously.

In-house shortcomings restraining informal industrialization

In the majority of cases the proprietor and manager of a small workshop is primarily an artisan, and male. He may have had some formal training, minimal in quality if not in time, or may have trained by apprenticeship, working in the workshop of someone else who is also likely to have had minimal training. The skill and technique basis of a small workshop is therefore unlikely to be broad or of a high quality. In the case of traditional indigenous craftsmen the skill level may be quite high by virtue of a genuine apprenticeship, usually within the extended family, but the technical scope is likely to be narrow.

While the owner's technical capability may be sufficient to carry out the production work successfully, he is most unlikely ever to have had any training in management, book-keeping or business strategies. Since administrative and managerial skills are essential if a small business is to thrive, their absence means that the majority of small workshops struggle on from hand to mouth, always risking collapse. In the case of one trained production engineer who runs a small metal fabrication workshop in Lusaka, Zambia, it became clear to an agency of the Development Bank that he was unaware of the difference between cash-flow and profit, with the result that his profitability was marginal and his loan repayments unreliable. Similarly, small businesses frequently approach this agency for loans for equipment which might allow them to diversify, in the mistaken belief that diversification is automatically the most profitable path (Schirra 1986). In the case of most rural artisans in Africa costings normally relate to time and materials only; the inclusion of profit and depreciation is not understood.

Given the technical and managerial limitations of workshop proprietors, and those of their employees, the habit of research and of sharing information within their peer group would make up for some of these deficiencies. Information is extremely hard to come by, and even where an advisory agency exists to provide it its expertise may be limited. Metalworking businesses which have asked for technical assistance have found that the theoretically trained young engineers who are sent to help them lack the practical knowledge which is essential in relation to a small workshop (Mulonga 1986). Business and financial advice appears to be more available than technical advice, which could be due partly to the perceptions of the agencies involved, partly to the ease of duplication and publishing of such information, and partly to the comparative difficulty of training competent technical extension workers. Knowledge and information are not, however, shared among workshops; indeed they are normally carefully guarded.

Even where an agency is offering assistance in this area the take-up is slow, since the idea of freely available information is alien. Traditionally an artisan's 'wisdom' is a precious thing, the birthright of his sons; if other children are allowed to know the secrets his sons will eventually be robbed of their inheritance, since their earnings will be lessened through competition. In the case of blacksmithing there are also traditional religious powers inherent in the activity, which encourage a further restriction. Such a tradition serves very well when the craftsman inherits the complete knowledge from his father, which is possible within the very limited requirements of traditional agriculture and village life. If, however, the inherited knowledge is incomplete, the second generation will lack some of the information and capability necessary to function satisfactorily within their working context. As the context within which the artisan functions changes and develops some old skills will become obsolete and disappear, for example, smelting ore for blacksmiths, but new skills and technologies must be acquired in turn if the trade in question is to remain relevant. The reluctance of many traditional indigenous craftsmen to change and adapt their ancestors' practices limits severely their usefulness in a developing environment. Where craftsmen are willing to adapt and develop their capabilities the only way in which such knowledge can reach the majority of small workshops is through a peer group grapevine; if this does not exist, as is the case in Zambia, for example, each workshop remains isolated and entirely reliant upon its own efforts for any development.

If techniques and designs relevant to contextual changes are to be developed, an indigenous design capability is necessary. While some work is being done in institutes worldwide on devising more appropriate technologies, and some of these may reach the field, in the vast majority of cases there remains a need for adaptation to local conditions. Local practitioners are best suited to this role, since they are intimately familiar with local requirements and conditions. In many cases appropriate technologies to meet the local needs have not been developed elsewhere, or if they have been are unlikely to have been transmitted to rural practitioners. In the case of artisans this applies equally to product designs appropriate to changing local requirements and to technologies and techniques appropriate to their own manufacturing process. While indigenous design and innovative capacity do exist among traditional artisans, their application and development are restricted by societal and physical factors. This restriction is a fundamental restraint upon the potential development of indigenous rural industry. Urban-oriented artisans whose technical training was institution based are less restricted in this way, but their usefulness tends to be correspondingly minimized by a lack of craftsmanship.

A small workshop in a developed country would normally have two choices when faced with the need for a process which it could not currently carry out in-house. The first is to acquire the necessary skills and equipment; access to these in Africa is generally problematic. The alternative is to forego the acquisition of the process and subcontract the work to another workshop which, while it may involve a cash outlay, conserves the workshop's inevitably limited capital resources and allows them to be concentrated more productively.

In Zambia and Zaire very little subcontracting between small workshops is to be found. Some subcontracting by big workshops to small ones does exist, but the subcontracting of work by small to large in order to obtain a component or a service which the small is unequipped to produce or undertake is rare. The result is that each workshop makes its own

14

products in their entirety, even where it lacks the equipment and/or the expertise to do so adequately. Resources committed to extending their capability in order to do this are often inadequate to finance the extension, and drain capital from elsewhere in the business.

The reasons given for the lack of subcontracting are doubts regarding delivery, quality and the honesty of the contractor. In the face of these a small workshop proprietor may often feel safer producing all components in-house, whatever the strain of doing so. In one case in Zambia a workshop was producing a component in-house for about 200 kwacha which could have been purchased from another manufacturer, at a better quality, for 20 kwacha (Siziba 1986).

Resource deficiencies which restrain informal industrialization

Four major resources are identified by artisans as being in short supply; credit, materials, transport and machinery. The lack of collateral and the lack of interest of banks in rural manufacturing enterprises is a major obstacle for artisanal entrepreneurs seeking credit, though growing recognition of the problem has finally led to attempts to address i realistically by some agencies. Aside from the basic problem of obtaining the necessary finance for equipment, loans are very expensive. For example, in 1986 a small (under £300) loan from Small-scale Enterprise Promotions Ltd (SEP) of the Development Bank of Zambia to a small workshop had to be repaid within six months at 24 per cent interest; even this rate of interest was less than commercial ones. At this time SEP made only 25 investment loans per year, which gives some indication of the difficulty small businesses face when seeking loans. Most capital equipment must be purchased abroad with foreign exchange, if it can be obtained; the rate of inflation in many developing countries means that by the time an apparently adequate amount of local currency has been collected it is likely to have become too devalued to pay the foreign exchange price of the goods. The problem of devalued currencies plagues development agencies as well as entrepreneurs (Schirra 1986).

Consumables are a continuous problem, particularly in countries with severe foreign exchange restrictions. In 1986 in Zambia, for example, foreign exchange was sold to commerce through a government auction system. The bulk of the US$4 million per week was taken by larger companies which were prepared to pay very high rates and to put up with the punishing conditions attached to the bidding and purchase. The small workshop could not compete in this market at all, and therefore had to rely on locally available materials and consumables (Lutzen 1986). If consumables are in short supply throughout the country, access to them in the rural areas is liable to pose enormous problems. One rural co-operative workshop which was visited in 1986 in Mpika, Zambia, was down to its last polished and almost toothless hacksaw blade, and had no other means of cutting metal. Subsequently the foreign exchange situation in Zambia worsened.

Raw materials are a problem mentioned by almost all small-scale manufacturers, particularly in the rural areas. The majority of small workshops, particularly those working in metal, exploit recycled material wherever possible, which adds to their economic virtue. New metal stock is difficult to come by; product lines are hard to standardize if the design must be altered for each individual item in order to accommodate the nature of the currently available material. Every aluminium foundry visited on one journey in Zambia and Zaire pointed out that its production was limited by the availability of scrap. The only hardened and special steels available to the small workshop are those found in vehicles; the most favoured parts are leaf springs, then torsion bars. In many rural blacksmiths' workshops the client must supply the steel from which the tool will be made, the problems of supply being too great for the smith to deal with himself. Little use appears to be made of coil springs and valves, though both would be ideal for chisels and some other edged tools. Timber is becoming increasingly expensive as deforestation advances, accelerated by the export of charcoal from forests to cities. Much of the carpentry in Mbuji-Mayi, Zaire, for example, is carried out with a plastic-laminated chipboard (Multiplex) manufactured in Kinshasa from timber cut elsewhere in the country (Tchimbangila 1986). Transport in the country is unreliable and expensive, which affects the supply of raw materials and therefore the fortunes of small workshops dependent upon new raw materials.

16

Material supply problems for small rural workshops whose raw materials are heavy are aggravated severely by transport difficulties. A smith from Manie, near Vanga, in Zaire, when offered a large quantity of material, could only accept one piece of truck chassis about one metre long, since this was the maximum he could carry the 20 or so kilometres back to his village; this would be sufficient for perhaps two days work. In this case he had also carried six heavy forged shovel blades the same distance in order to sell them. He was, however, nonetheless enthusiastic about the supply, which constituted a considerable improvement upon his normal situation. A commercial source of supply from this point, Lusekele, has now been established for the use of the local smiths. A great deal of the artisans' time can be wasted in unskilled ancillary tasks, restricting the energy available for production. The result is that materials delivered to and products collected from small workshops in remote villages are frequently sold and bought at exploitative prices by middle-men. A reed basket made in Manie and sold there earns its maker 30 zaires; the same basket sold in Kinshasa is worth 250 zaires.

In many cases the owners of workshops do hear of new technologies, and can recognize their possible relevance. Where in an industrial country this might lead to contact with a manufacturer of the relevant equipment, who would also supply any necessary information and back-up as part of the package, in a developing country this is unlikely to be the case. In the absence of off-the-shelf technology and equipment each workshop must construct the equipment or process itself either by 're-inventing the wheel' or, on the rare occasions that it can be obtained, from locally available information. Some simple workshop equipment is made locally within the informal sector, particularly in urban areas, but is limited and frequently of poor quality, such as the entirely home-made fixed-amperage arc welders made in Massina, Kinshasa, Zaire. These are made from scrap copper wire covered with brown paper, which is varnished before the wire is wrapped around home-made steel plates; the unit is used in open-air workshops without any casing, being stood on pieces of wood; the unswitched electrical connections are made by hand-twisting the wires to the mains supply. The use of such electrical equipment in a climate in which sudden downpours are the norm is not advised, though no deaths

17

were admitted to by the manufacturer. Even where the equipment can be purchased, though even a lathe may be made hand-made, the manner of using it must be developed in-house. The time required for such inefficient and generally low-level process and equipment development is likely to constitute a major drain on the energies and time of an innovative workshop. In the case of a workshop which is not capable of developing its own tools technological and product advance is likely to be minimal.

Even in cases where the capital with which to purchase equipment is available, the knowledge with which to analyse which process should be purchased and to identify the appropriate machine is generally absent. In developed countries such decisions are made with the assistance of the technical press, equipment salesmen and peer group, or consultants. In the case of a developing African country there is unlikely to be access to relevant technical publications; equipment salesmen are not sufficiently common, if they exist at all, to make a rational overview possible; and there is little or no communication with a peer group. In many cases the result is likely to be scarce resources spent on inappropriate equipment, to the detriment of the business.

General economic factors affect all businesses, but small workshops have limited resources and safety margins and are therefore more vulnerable to negative effects. In the same way, legislative measures designed to assist or protect another part of the economy may have unforeseen results for the informal sector, which does not have the muscle to promote its own favourable legislation. In order to promote agricultural development the government of Zambia removed all import duty on agricultural equipment in the 1980s, while continuing a 30 per cent tax on imports of steel. As a result of this, imported equipment, particularly from Zimbabwe, became far cheaper than the domestic product, the materials in Zambia sometimes costing as much as the imported finished item. The damage caused to the domestic implement manufacturing industry by this measure was enormous (Jonsson 1986). An environment protective and encouraging towards small workshops in particular and small enterprises in general is only likely to arise when such an approach becomes the basis of a national development policy. Where small enterprise is regarded as of minor economic significance it will always suffer from legislation and economic measures enacted with the modern sector in mind, these frequently being inappropriate to its needs and well-being. In an economy where foreign capital investment is encouraged the informal sector is also liable to be disadvantaged by competition from the resulting import-substitution products and by the domination of the modern-sector bias of such policies.

Rural industrial viability

Unstable local conditions and the rapidly varying effects of international trade concerning developing countries mean that central African rural industry exists in a context of continual change. Few factors are constant, even within the general field of rural industry where the sources of skills, stages of evolution, orientations and purposes differ widely.

Rural industrialization almost invariably means small informal workshops, a large proportion of which do not provide the sole occupation of their workers. While some categories of workshop can be established, elision is normal and distinctions are generally blurred. While a cash economy is more and more dominant, there is still considerable trade by barter in rural areas, although, for example, this is illegal in Zaire (Selig 1987). Among such non-cash transactions there may also be social obligations operating to the direct economic disadvantage of the artisan which, being a significant component of the social structure, are therefore nonetheless worth maintaining (Mbwa 1988). Within the group culture of a village, profit alone is not the motivating force; social relationships and dynamics also have a strong effect. The majority of the rural population continues to be involved in agriculture, most of its subsistence requirements being produced locally. However, the demands of the cash economy increase continually the need for either cash-crop production or the generation of non-agricultural income.

The viability of rural industries generally reflects the economic level of the community within which those industries exist; it is frequently difficult, therefore, to establish the underlying potential of an industry (or of a single workshop or artisan). The decline of an industry may occur through strangulation because of inadequate infrastructure, because of official repression (Muller 1980), or because it is genuinely obsolete. A change in the conditions of production, such as infrastructural development, favourable government policy or complementary development, may dramatically alter the prognosis for such an industry. For example, an unpublished paper relating to a rural mechanization pilot project in the Central Province of Zambia states that

> From a tour that was undertaken by Mr Mukutu to Refunsa and Chungwe, visiting craftsmen, one point that emerged was that the prospects for village metalworking are very limited unless there are working oxen. Once there are working oxen in the area the prospects expand enormously. (Zambia 1979)

(Since the oxen are used to pull carts, ploughs and sometimes harrows, the demand for metal product and repairs is usually increased when animal traction is introduced.)

There is a tendency to regard traditional occupations as obsolete by definition, and to concentrate development initiatives upon 'new' industries. Not only is this to disregard a valuable resource, but the expensive replacement of it is likely to become necessary, even though the context, and therefore the problems, will remain essentially the same. The stability, demise or expansion of a rural industry should not be regarded as an isolated phenomenon, nor should its worth be judged solely upon its current performance. Newly introduced rural industries, such as motor mechanics and welding, have a greater potential economic viability than their traditional counterparts because they deal directly with the mechanical representations of the cash economy and of the more industrialized urban centres. However, rather than benefiting the local economy they may constitute part of the threat to it, by sustaining an import-export economy rather than supporting autarkic development.

While rural development is not only concerned with agriculture, farming is the major economic activity in any rural area and is therefore the one that should be developed initially, particularly since the commodities produced by it are fundamental to survival. Since agriculture is the dominant rural economic activity it is also the principal market available to any small workshop, until such time as a broadening local economy creates new ones.

The first industrial requirements for the support of agriculture are wood and metal workshops capable of limited production of tools and equipment, and of their repair. Once these have been established, exploiting the agricultural economy to finance their existence, they are then available for the manufacture of other, non-agricultural products. Their principal role should be that of producing and repairing capital goods, goods to be used in the production of commodities and the execution of services such as agricultural and artisanal tools. The wood and metal workshops' capacities constitute a basic resource for the equipping of all kinds of local enterprise; their existence is vital to rural industrialization and economic expansion.

Industrial origins: traditional or implanted?

Rural manufacturing industries are artisan based. The knowledge of the artisans is likely to derive from either Northern or traditional sources.

Artisans trained in the urban modern sector or through organized technical training schemes may acquire an extensive technical repertoire, but, because of the dichotomy between their training and the rural society in which they exist, such artisans may be regarded as implanted. Included in this category are the subsequent apprentices of the original implanted trainees.

Traditional artisans regard their knowledge as inherited wisdom, an integral part of their lives and their place in society. This is particularly true of blacksmithing, which in many places still retains some of its traditional religious significance.

The general difference in the quality of output between traditional and implanted artisans appears to have a philosophical basis, since the actions of the implanted artisan have no connection with the rest of his life other than the provision of money, while the knowledge of the traditional artisan is regarded as wisdom, has come from his fathers and is to be protected. Skills and understandings acquired by such a route carry with them a sense of quality. Where technical capability has been taught to a group of trainees with a limited goal in mind, generally the production of a restricted range of products which have no personal connection to the maker, the accent has been on economy of training, on making a machine of the trainee in order that the limited task can be performed. This is the normal Northern approach to training, but in most examples seen in central Africa even this training has been abbreviated as far as possible, principally in the interests of economy. While limited goal

21

training may satisfy the immediate apparent need for which the artisan is being schooled, in the long run neither the community nor the trainee benefits, since the paucity of the experience fails to equip the artisan with the ability to adapt to future requirements, to take a pride in his capacity and therefore exercise a sense of quality. In essence, Northern training has been passing on the Northern industrial disease of lack of interest and depersonalization to the new generations of African craftsmen providing poor material from which a general technological base must be built.

The alien nature of much of the implanted training frequently involves the use of modern equipment, as at the Institute Technique Professionel in Kikwit, Zaire, which apart from requiring very substantial capital also demands the use of electricity. Even in Kikwit, a substantial town, electricity supplies are uncertain, there being normally none during the day and frequently none at night either, while in rural areas they simply do not exist. Thus any implanted artisan whose training involves the use of electrically powered equipment must remain in an urban environment, or re-learn his trade. One man trained at Kikwit, Mr Mudi Kosi, requested blacksmithing training from the smiths trained at Manie, since in order to get work with his Kikwit skills he had had to move to Kinshasa, but wished to return to his rural home. Implanted training schemes are of little relevance to rural industrialization, except where the training has been specifically tailored to local needs and limitations. Although there have been some successes in the centralized training of rural craftsmen, as at the Selima Trade School in Malawi, there is also evidence that the subsequently implanted artisans do not always adapt very well to their rural practice, not least because they are often located in communities remote from their own extended family. In addition, even where technical training is appropriate to rural practice, and is carried out in the rural environment, the context of the training remains Northern, in terms of substantial purpose-built workshops and imported industrially produced tools. While the individuals trained in this environment may be able to adapt to less pretentious village facilities they have nonetheless received the suggestion that a 'proper' workshop requires a capital-intensive building which is inappropriate to village establishment, and unnecessary in relation to the initial products of such workshops. Ox-traction equipment can be built in conventional local workshops, with locally made tools. Where, as in the case of the Oxfam-funded projects in the Kasai, Zaire, sets of blacksmithing equipment were imported from England (Crighton 1986) the implication is that it is not possible to duplicate the workshop without similar expensive imports. By contrast, the two books by Aaron Moore containing instructions for making a total of nineteen woodworking tools are expressly designed for the independent local exploitation and are appropriate for use in rural or urban environments, provided the carpenter using them can read English (Moore 1986–7).

If the function of a rural primary workshop is to further the development of other local enterprise, including agriculture, establishing the means to provide must be a high priority. A sophisticated workshop with a skilled staff capable of dealing with all eventualities may appear to be the resource required, but is totally unrealistic in a developing country with minimal funds available, even if the necessary skills already existed.

> The idea has to be accepted that each of the 6000 villages in Tanzania eventually will need a metal workshop (blacksmith, mechanic) and a woodworking workshop (carpenter) if agricultural mechanization and better animal husbandry is to find a secure and broad base (Kienbaum, in Muller 1980).

While such a conclusion is logical, the means by which the goal is achieved, and the cost of doing so, is crucial to the reality of the proposal:

> However, although the (Kienbaum) report recommends that these workshops should employ existing craftsmen, it also estimates that each pair of workshops should be provided with tools, equipment and working capital worth 120,000 T.shs (15,000 US$), i.e., 72,000 T.shs for the blacksmith workshop and 48,000 T.shs for the carpenter workshop, and each should receive extension service and advice costing a similar amount of money.
>
> These sums of money are extraordinarily high. In case this implied standard of workshops should be accepted and introduced as the general conception of a village workshop for all the 6000 villages mentioned, it would be detrimental to the whole idea. It would cost about 14 million. T.shs (or almost 1% of the current total development budget for the whole country) to establish just 60 pairs of workshops *per year*, and it would take 100 years to 'cover' the country (assuming that the number of villages remains constant). (Muller 1980)

If it is accepted that the development of rural economic activities of all kinds depends upon the existence of primary workshops, yet that the cost of such workshops is prohibitive, the equation necessary for rural development would appear to be insoluble. However, the conventional Northern concept of a workshop, upon which Kienbaum's estimates of cost appear to be based, bears little relation to the rural African norm which must form the foundation of local primary workshops.

If the number of primary workshops is to be sufficient to have a significant effect, such workshops must be established independently, from local resources, since the scale of the problem is beyond centralized funding. Since the cost of conventional (generally imported) tools and equipment limits severely the range of facilities which any workshop can hope to achieve, alternative means of acquiring equipment and of carrying out technical processes must be found. The development of a workshop's capability to supply itself with tools and technical expertise is fundamental to its ability to develop with minimal external support.

The traditional artisan, besides the philosophical virtues of his training, exists already in a social and economic structure of which he is an integral part and to which his training is directly related. Since it is this very social and economic micro-system which, among many others, requires development, the most logical vehicle for rural industrialization is the traditional artisan. This is not to suggest that such artisans are perfectly equipped to play the desired role, but if ways can be found to develop their knowledge appropriately, particularly in agriculture, success is far more likely than by means of implanted artisans, since the traditionals have already demonstrated their motivation and staying power, and their ability to operate under existing limitations.

2. Rural workshops

The comparative viability of urban and rural informal manufacturing

> Their production processes are characterized by a low capital-labour ratio. For our economy where capital is scarce and labour abundant this fact is an important consideration. Secondly, small-scale production is often the only means of meeting demand when the size of the market for any given item is small. This is particularly the case for relatively isolated markets in small towns and rural areas. These enterprises can, therefore, play a useful role in programmes of industrial decentralization. Thirdly, they help in the tapping of resources such as entrepreneurship, capital, and raw materials which otherwise would remain unused. They generally mobilize family or community savings which might have remained idle or been spent on unproductive activities. (*Kenya 1979*)

ONE OF THE COMMONEST and most severe constraints upon small-scale manufacturing activity is a shortage of inputs. In the case of metalworkers, working largely with scrapmaking, the principal source of raw material is urban-based industry and consumers. The consequent shortage of scrap in rural areas means that many blacksmiths are dependent upon their customers to supply the material with which they work, which results in a far lower income than if they had direct access to the metal themselves. In the case of the Manie blacksmiths, when clients provide the material the products made from it are shared equally between smith and client, resulting in 40 per cent lower earnings than if the smith's own material is used. By contrast urban metalworkers have access to a comparatively reliable supply of metal from scrap vehicles and other recycled sources. The density of the urban environment makes it economical for them to search out metal directly themselves, or to take advantage of the scrap dealers who can exist due to the level of informal metalworking activity. If there is any new metal stock available for purchase the urban manufacturer is in a good position to get it; where material supplies are restricted they are unlikely to be available to the rural artisan. For example, tinsmiths in urban Zimbabwe have normally been able to use new metal sheet, imported from South Africa by the formal sector, while rural tinsmiths are restricted almost exclusively to recycled sheets of frequently inappropriate gauge. Further differences in the availability of tools and the quality of peer group practice result in the rural practitioners being largely dependent upon repair work, while their urban counterparts concentrate upon new products, which is a more profitable activity (Cromwell and Harries1989). Urban artisans also have better access to other processed inputs, particularly consumables such as nails, sandpaper, hacksaw blades and tools in general.

The means of production available to small-scale manufacturers are also considerably affected by location. Access to electricity is most unusual in rural areas, whereas it is becoming increasingly common in urban centres, even if it is not always reliable. The availability of electricity, a reasonably cheap and versatile source of power, can dramatically change the quality of finish, the processes, and the speed of production possible. The presence of other related expertise also means that some repair of such capital equipment is possible. In metalworking, access to welding capacity (or the lack of it) affects the product range that is possible, and can also give significant price advantages to the products concerned. In addition to this, consumers generally prefer to buy goods which they believe have been made by modern means. However, there are also negative effects, since mechanized processes often require less skill of the artisan and therefore, particularly in the case of welding, allow poor quality goods a cosmetic attraction. While in many places this has resulted in the blacksmiths losing the hoe as a product to a combination of industrial and welded urban manufactures, it is interesting to note that in rural Zimbabwe at least some farmers prefer the blacksmith-made hoe for its durability, in spite of slightly higher cost. The adaptation of industrially produced hoes to suit local soil conditions is a further service which the smiths provide (Cromwell 1989). Factory-made hoes are not always cheaper; in South-eastern Tanzania in 1991 blacksmith-made hoes cost approximately half the price of the industrial product, and dominated the market.

All manufacturing activity is dependent upon the market for its products. While some rural manufacturers have specific advantages, such as a direct relationship with rural customers and a personal understanding of their requirements, the size of the market and its spending power are of major significance. An urban market with comparatively strong spending power is able to buy a diverse range of products in considerable quantities throughout the year, creating many opportunities for the local artisan. In contrast spending power in rural areas is limited, cash being scarce except for a brief post-harvest period, if the harvest has been adequate. The low spending power limits severely the range of products which can be sold, while the lower density of the population restricts the size of the individual artisan's market.

Most rural artisanal manufacture and repair is combined with subsistence farming, allowing access to cash for external purchases and such formal sector costs as school fees and taxes. Even where an artisan has access to credit, permitting business expansion and increased productivity, where raw material is available, the local rural market is unlikely to be able to support those additional costs. Urban artisans, on the other hand, are normally in a far better position to expand their production since their greater market is more likely to be able to provide the revenue for this. The possibilities for access to credit are likely to be better in an urban environment. Where the transport infrastructure is good the position of rural artisans is further eroded by competition from urban manufacturers.

Where the development of small enterprise is being contemplated by an external agent the possibilities are likely to be more easily measurable and on a considerably larger scale in the urban environment than in the rural one. The convenience of working in a more accessible area and the far lower cost of advisory inputs are additional attractions. Urban enterprises are more likely to benefit from, and thus repay loans for, improvements in capital equipment, a consistently favoured technological solution to enterprise development. In addition, the apparent returns from the amount of effort required for rural enterprise development seem very limited because of the part-time commitment of the majority of practitioners, compared to the full-time professional involvement of the urban entrepreneur. This full-time activity is perceived as more valuable and laudable by

27

the majority of external agents to whom full-time specialized activity is the norm. Subsistence farmers who do a little manufacturing on the side are generally not perceived as making a significant contribution to rural development, and are considered to be unrewarding as a subject for input in terms of quantifiable results. The majority of loans to small businesses from such agencies as SEDOM in Malawi or the Small Industries Development Organization (SIDO) in Zambia go to urban or peri-urban enterprises; extensive rural credit support is only likely to arise where that is the specific focus of the agency involved.

Where most of the production and marketing conditions favour the urban manufacturer, it is to be expected that initiatives to develop urban small manufacturing enterprise have been far more successful than those aimed at the rural equivalent. The most notable example of urban small-scale enterprise development is the growth of manufacturing activity at Suame Magazine, Ghana, which was imaginatively supported by the Technology Consultancy Centre, Kumasi (Smillie 1986), through business development and the introduction of intermediate products and services which enabled faster businesses to be set up. The Magazine is now the centre of the vehicle repair trade in Ghana, as well as encompassing a range of other manufacturing and repair activities, particularly in metal; several thousand people are currently employed. Aluminium casting has already been referred to and is an example of an activity which has spread widely in a number of urban centres in Africa, but which is dependent upon a raw material, scrap aluminium, found almost exclusively in the urban context. Some work has been done to assist and develop the activity, for example by Oxfam in Kinshasa, but, like any commercially viable low-capital cost activity in an urban environment, it has tended to spread of its own accord. Such casting, while it can be carried out manually, is greatly assisted by an electrically powered rotary fan. Not only is the urban commercial environment more appropriate for such activities than that in rural areas; but the lack of agricultural opportunities in the cities means that people are entirely dependent upon direct income generation. Since unemployment is high and rising in most African countries the attraction of informal-sector activity is considerable in urban areas. The potential for a fruitful relationship between an urban entrepreneur and a development agency is reasonably good where continuity is comparatively easy to achieve and constraints are limited to those affecting the whole economy. The input made by the Development Technology Unit of Warwick University to Mr Siziba's metal fabrication business in Lusaka assisted considerably in his ability to develop products, the business being further enabled by a substantial loan from the SEP section of the Development Bank of Zambia. It is in fact significant that the problems occurring within Mr Siziba's business centred around the many choices open to him and his reluctance to concentrate more profitably upon a limited number of product lines, instead of diffusing his energies and capital by custom-building a wide range of products. His business demonstrates that, with the right inputs, skills and support profitable small-scale businesses are entirely feasible in urban and peri-urban areas.

Examples of successful small-scale manufacturing enterprise arising from external interventions in rural areas are much harder to find. The difficulty continually encountered in material supply, the limitations of the market and what it will support, the predominantly part-time nature of artisanal activity and the frequently misplaced expectations of external agents' interventions make success unusual. If an agency attempts to develop a rural manufacturing enterprise along conventional lines, which are essentially urban, they are unlikely to be successful. It is no accident that by far the largest proportion of rural business loans provided in Zambia, for example, is to finance hammer mills with which the staple food is processed (Schirra 1986). Milling is one of the few rural services which are not seasonal and which is economically viable for the whole community. However, although hammer-mills benefit the community by easing the work load of women, they bring no cash into the village, but instead require cash outflow to pay for the machinery, diesel and spares. The conditions of rural manufacturing differ significantly from the urban equivalent, and this must be recognized if an intervention is to be effective and sustainable. The author of a detailed and careful survey of non-agricultural enterprise in the communal lands in Zimbabwe (Helmsing 1987) went to considerable pains to quantify the value of rural blacksmiths' work and their activity, and came to the conclusion that the smiths were making a loss. This assertion was arrived at by allocating a value to the smiths' time, and costing their work accordingly. To apply such measures is to ignore the special context of the activity, the reasons for undertaking it and the results desired by the practitioner and will inevitably create mistaken beliefs. A subsistence farmer who also makes some forged items for his own use and for sale is on the edge of the cash economy. His principal needs are catered for by the family's farming activities, which do not have a direct cash value since the products are required largely for domestic consumption. Yet cash is required for agricultural inputs and domestic requirements such as school fees, certain foodstuffs and consumer items, and, being difficult to acquire within the local rural economy, has a value above the exchange value of equivalent agricultural produce. For example, an axe and a chicken may have the same value, but the smith would sooner be paid in cash than with the chicken, since the need he is trying to meet is for cash. In many cases the farmer will only make sufficient products to meet his cash requirement, other than responding to the demands of his immediate customers. Even if the cash takes longer to earn than the equivalent in local goods it is justifiable and useful to do so in order to obtain access to the external inputs required for agriculture and the home. Beyond that point the benefit of working at a loss diminishes, so extensive production becomes less worthwhile. Helmsing suggests that the agricultural activities subsidize the artisanal production, but the reverse is true; the artisanal activities are undertaken at a lower apparent return in order to supply the necessary external inputs for the agriculture, which require cash (Cromwell and Harries 1989).

The result of such misleading measurement is that either the subjects will not be regarded as suitable for assistance or that the assistance given will be misconceived, usually attempting to change the activity into one more recognizably urban, where Northern-influenced expectations are more likely to be met. However, the results are more frequently an apparent lack of interest and a failure to capitalize upon the inputs made, leading to the assumption that the failure is the fault of the artisan rather than the input. A blacksmithing project carried out in Malawi attempted to raise considerably the technical level of rural blacksmithing, involving a significant increase in the capital levels required. The majority of part-time smiths failed to respond, probably because the changes introduced to the activity were too extreme to be

30

undertaken at one step, and because the motivation to extend their activities was not matched by sufficient need, as described above for the Zimbabwean smiths (ITDG 1989).

To use conventional business measurement to conclude that rural small-scale business is inherently unviable leads to the conclusion that the practitioner does not know what she or he is doing. The extent of the knowledge of farmers and indigenous rural practitioners of various kinds is now widely recognized as pertinent and well-tuned to local conditions. The viability of an activity can only be gauged if its full context is understood, just as the limits of the extent to which it is viable may only be judged if the need it is intended to meet is acknowledged. The fundamental purpose of traditional rural manufacturing activity is to support subsistence agriculture and, as part of that, the domestic existence of the farmers. The development of rural manufacturing will only succeed where this purpose is recognized and reinforced. This means that interventions which concern themselves with the income of the practitioner rather than the perceived needs of the community and the practitioner are inherently unviable.

The significance of innovation

Traditional practices such as blacksmithing can easily become marginalized by the incursion of industrially produced goods or welded artifacts from urban areas, where access to scrap steel is much easier; conversely, the decline of a national economy usually has an extreme effect upon formal-sector industry and the urban artisans' advantages are diminished by declines in the transport infrastructure. Since the economies of the majority of African countries are under pressure the comparative advantages of the rural artisans are often no longer diminishing, while their function within their communities increases in significance once more.

Fluctuations in the market position of the rural artisans make the ability to respond to changes in demand for different products essential. Market opportunities are generally limited, making access to those which do exist very important. The small number of alternative products which can be made results from a combination of the limited seasonal purchasing capacity of rural communities, the degree of penetration from formal and urban manufacturers and the level of competition they offer in terms of price and quality, and the severe technical and infrastructural restrictions within which rural artisans work.

While the artisans' ability to make products wherever an opportunity exists is important to her or his own survival, it is even more important to the community within which they work, since an opportunity for the artisan represents an unsatisfied need of the local consumers. This is particularly true of repair services, which are rarely if ever available from remote manufacturers. Repair services do not, however, constitute by themselves a sufficient market opportunity for an artisan since they are almost invariably less profitable than manufacturing, normally requiring more input for less return. The exceptions are specific repair activities relating to items of great strategic value such as bicycles.

In order to be able to take advantage of varying market opportunities and to survive variations in available resources the ability to make the best possible use of raw materials and tools is of fundamental importance. If an artisan is unable to innovate then the workshop's capability remains static. Since the context is far from static such an artisan is vulnerable, and becomes increasingly unable to maintain the service which the community either does require at the present time, or may need in the future. Finding ways to circumvent the lack of particular equipment or materials and to maximize the usefulness of those which do exist is of fundamental significance to the rural manufacturer and repairer.

In developed countries an artisan has access to information concerning materials and means of production, in a context of plentiful supply. In Africa an artisan is faced with a general unavailability of inputs and an almost total lack of information about the ways in which change can be accommodated or taken advantage of. With rare exceptions technical and design development must be originated by the practitioner. Though there is some potential for the sharing of knowledge between practitioners, the tradition of the protection of knowledge as a valuable commodity militates against it in many areas. In addition, almost all artisans are in the same position, their knowledge relating to existing practices, usually coming from a traditional base. In this way there is only a limited possibility of an established practitioner gaining assistance in developing adaptations or innovation from a more able peer.

In the majority of rural workshops in Africa production is not systematic. While the limited number of products could be considered as 'lines', goods are normally made on an individual basis. Exceptions to this are unusual and quite dramatic, as at Phalula in Malawi where a group of smiths who mainly make axes produces them in batches, maximizing the use of time and fuel. In contrast the majority of smiths, including those at Manie, make one axe at a time, from start to finish, even if there are several to be made. Whenever a new product or a variation is required, design input is necessary. The general use of scrap material by blacksmiths also demands a capacity to vary even a standard product slightly according to the form of the raw material. Repairs consistently make demands on the design capability of the artisan, since breakage may occur in many ways. Even where an article breaks regularly in a similar way, recognizing and adapting to variations is necessary, for example in the repairing of large Chinese enamel bowls with rusted out bottoms, as is done in Zaire. Solving problems and innovating within existing parameters is an essential part of the activity, even when additional adaptation and innovation are not necessitated by changing external factors.

The level of innovation of which a rural workshop is capable varies greatly throughout the continent, depending upon the cultural tradition, the education and training systems through which the practitioner has learned both technical and intellectual habits, the extent of their confidence in their skills, and the time available to them to do the experimentation necessary for innovation. Attitudes to risk-taking are also of fundamental significance: the more marginal the economy of the community, the greater the caution regarding risk will usually be.

Innovation involves taking risks, since the outcome of a particular innovative course of action is invariably uncertain. To be willing to take risks and to be able to deal with the consequences of failure, the artisan needs a reasonable level of professional confidence.

To experiment in order to find possible ways of doing things and to test the application of such ideas demands time. Such 'industrial leisure' can only be created by the generation of a surplus income which allows for the not immediately productive use of time and materials for experimentation. Before innovation can become a regular feature of an artisan's activity, the point where such a surplus can be created must be reached and an awareness of the need to re-invest it in the activity must exist.

While the author was working with the smiths of Manie in 1987 he explored their attitude to undertaking innovation. Because the entire craft had been learned from their elders and was seen as coming from their ancestors, it was not based upon analysis and experiment. For those who had had primary education this attitude had been further inhibited by a system of learning by rote which leaves little to individual initiative. The group culture is also heavily prejudiced against individual advantage, so experiment in order to gain such advantage is not acceptable to the larger group. The principal smith, Waka Ngai, is believed to have been poisoned by others of his clan early in 1989 because he was not felt to be sharing enough of the economic benefits which they believed him to have gained through working with the foreign blacksmith (Selig 1989). Even in less extreme cases the accumulation of surplus as capital or even working capital is extremely difficult, since any cash or kind would immediately be annexed by other members of the extended family. For example, one smith, Ada, had no money with which to buy the steel that he needed and which was briefly available in the village, because all the cash he possessed had been used by his family to purchase a child's dress the previous day.

In order to test the smiths' ability to design in response to demand a very simple problem, the design of a cracker for oil-palm nuts, was presented, causing considerable unease. One group of younger smiths did attempt a solution, but were unable to test it because of a lack of steel with which to experiment. It was the firm opinion of the smiths in general that any available material from which commercial products could be realized should be reserved solely for that purpose. The young smiths had no leeway in the matter, making any product development even more difficult for them.

The use of time for innovation constituted a major risk, since the smiths barely survive on their output. The time taken to work with the researcher was a major investment and was carefully limited in order to minimize the cost. The work done was almost exclusively on items which they saw knowledge of as an urgent need and which they had directly requested, so the connection between cost and benefit was immediate and obvious in their minds. Even so, there were

34

comparatively few smiths who could afford to participate for all the sessions, though the pressure to do so grew as the recognition of the potential benefits increased.

It is difficult to know precisely why there was so little confidence to experiment, since the absence of opportunity effectively prevents any practice of doing so, complicating the other factors involved. What was clear was that any significant advance in the development of products was made quite remote because of a lack of confidence and the consequent reluctance to take risks with scarce resources. This does not negate the work which was done with these smiths, since the most urgent need was to consolidate their activities so that the subsistence farming community should retain access to their services. The priority identified by them was the making of tools for their own use, which served this purpose.

Sustainability and growth

The interests of the African communities in which small-scale manufacturing enterprises exist generally require that they be sustained for the sake of the services they supply. This should be a primary concern of any external agent working in this field. Where existing enterprises are concerned it will initially be a question of consolidation rather than development. However, the person with the greatest interest in the sustainability of the enterprise is the entrepreneur, so client-orientation on the part of external agents will prioritize this fundamental goal. Any failure to protect the sustainability risks the demise of the enterprise, losing the income for those working in it and the benefits of its services for the local community, and so defeating the purposes of the external agent. The greatest threat to sustainability when external agents intervene is the introduction of artificial solutions to persistent problems which the practitioner will be unable to maintain following the departure of the external agent's influence. The use of the agent's transport or agent-influenced market links are frequent examples of this.

The principal factors considered to affect the initial viability of small workshops are the availability of:

o Investment capital
o Working capital

- o Accessible markets
- o Appropriate infrastructure
- o Raw materials
- o Tools, equipment and consumables
- o Management and technical skills
- o Suitable products or services
- o Motivation.

The level of available resources necessary for the establishment of a small workshop varies widely, as do the quality and scale of the commercial competition. In the most extreme case the possession of simple skills may constitute the vital resource, for example where capital equipment is a pair of pliers and raw material is some scrap wire for the production of toys for a market devoid of them. Even at this level all factors can be quantified, since they must be present in some form for the enterprise to exist. While the minute scale of the factors might be considered to lessen the importance of each element, the problems are equally great for the artisan at every level, since the scale of operation is a reflection of the available resources.

The relative importance of the different factors is variable, as a workshop can be operated on minimal availability of one or more resources if these are compensated for by a strength in others. Poor infrastructure, for example, is less relevant if an adequate market is available locally, if tools and consumables are home-made, and if raw materials are either home produced or easily available. Capital requirement is minimal under these conditions compared to the need for skill, as is management expertise.

Just as all the factors listed above affect the fundamental existence of a small workshop, so the resources they demand must be appropriately augmented if the workshop is to grow. As the scale of the workshop develops, the balance between the various factors increases in importance, quickly passing the point where a strength in one area can compensate sufficiently for a weakness in another. At any stage in development, inadequacy in the resources with which to deal with any one factor might be identified as the principal impediment, but it is essential to recognize that all factors must be responded to in the appropriate degree at all stages of the workshop's development. While the proportional relationship may vary, for example ample investment capital and the corresponding equipment may bring about a lessening of the skill requirement, each factor continues to be essential for the workshop's development.

A workshop can be established with the resources required to deal with the factors listed above alone, and may indeed be able to develop to a certain extent without the contribution of any other resource. If, however, development is to proceed at a reasonable pace and progress to a significant extent four further essentials are needed:

o Skill acquisition
o Information availability
o Analytical decision making
o Design

It would be wrong to suppose that these resources would not make valuable contributions to the enterprise from the very first but in many cases a workshop will be producing traditional or standard products or services using traditional or standard resources and practices for which minimal innovation is required.

For the development of a small workshop an expansion of capability is essential, whether in management, technology, or product development. The knowledge necessary for this expansion can either be original or received.

Subjects upon which a small workshop may require information include:

o Obtaining finance
o Regulations and laws

o Markets
o Product patterns

o Material technology
o Material sources
o Technology
o Technology sources and choice

Subjects upon which a small workshop may require instructional material include:

o Management
o Book keeping
o Marketing
o Techniques and skill development

The availability of information and instructional material allows capability to increase without recourse to costly empirical development, although selection decisions are still essential. If information on all areas of concern is not available universal improvization becomes unavoidable, in many cases leading to less than satisfactory solutions, since such solutions will always be first stage rather than a development of accumulated wisdom.

While capital, equipment and raw materials frequently present difficulties, most information will probably come originally from a source external to the locality, since technological and business levels are likely to be generally low, making useful peer group assistance minimal. In addition to this, the traditions of keeping 'wisdom' within the family militates against a mutually supportive attitude to the sharing of information among peers. Many small workshops in Africa identify a lack of information as a considerable constraint. The instructional material which they believe they require relates to methods of technical improvization, techniques, product design, finance or marketing. It is frequently true that they lack even information regarding resources available within their own locality, such as might be provided by other small workshops or formal agencies (Siziba 1986).

Acquiring information in any society is time-consuming and expensive, the results depending to a considerable extent upon the level of knowledge of the seeker. In the African small workshop context the seeker is therefore normally the most skilled and knowledgeable person in the workshop, who will normally be the owner and also the key worker. Given the paucity of information resources, the uncertain gain which results from a certain loss of output is a doubtful incentive to the commitment of time and money. Since small workshops frequently operate on narrow subsistence margins, where the shortage of cash correspondingly increases the significance of the time that any task requires, a spontaneous seeking out of information is likely to be an exercise which it is only rarely possible to carry out. Once a workshop has grown to the point where the owner is no longer required to be continually working at the bench, but is largely concerned with management functions, some of her/his liberated time can be dedicated to the gathering of useful information; this may indeed be regarded as part of the function of a manager. At this stage the workshop would pass beyond our definition of small, that is, that full-time management is not required, the owner still being 'dirty-handed'.

The smaller the workshop the more vital is the need for information and instructional material, but the harder it is to acquire it. In rural areas geographical isolation exacerbates the problem considerably.

Form of design input required by primary and secondary workshops

Whatever the developmental context of a small workshop and whatever the level of sophistication it achieves, there will always be a design requirement. The consumption of design input is likely to increase as the workshop grows, and the nature of the input is also likely to change. Initially the requirement will be for solutions to problems of a shortage of resources with which to make and repair conventional products previously designed elsewhere. As the workshop grows and its resources increase, the emphasis is likely to change to product design, with less time required for the development of the means of production by design and innovation, particularly if the workshop is a specialist one.

A definitive categorization of primary and secondary workshops is unrealistic, since many workshops will play a dual role or move from one category to the other. Even where both functions are carried out in the same workshop, however, the differing design requirements will generally apply to each activity.

A primary workshop is design intensive. Flexibility, being able to originate or develop, produce and repair a wide variety of products for different activities, requires separate design input for almost every job, with the full range of decisions regarding function, form, construction, materials and processes being taken each time. In addition, although process development and innovation to redress workshop deficiencies are required in both primary and secondary shops, there will be far more of this necessary in a primary workshop because of the variety of tasks it will undertake; in a secondary workshop, once the product range and the means of manufacture or repair are established, the need for everyday design input is minimized, as output and the activity become increasingly standardized.

A secondary workshop is production intensive. Although

continual shop-floor problem solving is not required in secondary workshops concerned with the production of standardized goods, more specialized long-term input is required for product design and development, and for the development of processes appropriate to the production of those products. Cosmetic design input is also required for consumer products, whereas the capital goods of the primary workshop will largely succeed or fail on function and price alone at this level of market.

As a result of the wide variety of products and repairs of which a primary workshop must be capable, little standardization or specialism is possible. All tools and capital equipment must have the widest possible application; high-cost tools must be employed continually in order to justify themselves; a specialist tool can only be justified by a specialist output. In the context of a rural African small workshop any tool may be regarded as being high-cost, and therefore must be broadly useful in a primary workshop situation.

Just as each tool or item of equipment must be as broadly applicable as possible, so the workers in a primary workshop must be able to cope with all the design and production problems which arise. Design must take place at a shop-floor level, and each worker must be capable of the necessary decision-making. While some decisions can be taken centrally by the owner or manager, the degree to which input is necessary makes the capability a general requirement. The scarcity of such workers reinforces the case for a separation of roles between primary and secondary shops, so that primary workshops with skilled designer-workers do not waste this resource on standardized production tasks.

Since tasks are individualized, most design input is job-specific, and must therefore be undertaken by the worker carrying out the task; there is little external design input possible regarding shop-floor activity in primary workshops. In the same way the potential for input in terms of designs of tools and equipment for the workshop's own use is limited, since the manufacture of items such as a metal-bending machine (ITDG 1972) represents a considerable investment to the workshop for a tool which, although applicable to many products, is still comparatively specialist in function, and would therefore only rarely be undertaken even where the workshop is aware of the design.

Locally available extension services giving relevant design

advice would be a desirable resource for the workshop, but the cost would be enormous. Since design input is a continuous requirement, reliance cannot be placed on any outside agency to provide it; the capability must be found in the workshop. It is also arguable that the valuable resource of capable workers should be applied directly, running their own workshops, rather than being employed as advisers for an expensive extension service of questionable overall effectiveness.

The principal external design contribution which can be made to primary workshops is the provision of appropriate designs for capital goods which the shop may be required to make for local use by various types of secondary enterprises. An example of this approach in the UK, in the area of consumer goods (decorative ironwork), is the CoSIRA pattern book for blacksmiths, a book of varied designs for use by blacksmiths which has been very widely used in the past, often directly as a pattern book for customer selection, though its use is now diminishing as its decorative designs become increasingly dated. The work of the Intermediate Technology Development Group (ITDG) with ApT (Appropriate Technology Design and Development) in producing detailed manuals for the production of metalworking items and other equipment (ITDG 1972) is a good example of this approach, which could be employed usefully over a wider range of capital products. Dissemination of the design material, and the best form for such material, remains a problem. The publication of separate booklets for each item of equipment may keep the individual cost down but makes the acquisition by each small workshop of a design reference library extremely difficult and highly unlikely. Past attempts at bringing a number of designs together have been unsatisfactory in various ways, most commonly in the professionalism and clarity of their presentation (Macpherson 1975).

One of the best known (VITA 1975) suffers from being so eclectic as to be of little use to any particular shop; it is reputed to include designs which have never been properly tested. Published manuals, of a type standard in the North, require literacy and the ability to read engineering drawings, which immediately restricts the number of African workshops in which they can be used. ITDG has begun to use technical illustration to convey technical information, with promising results.

41

A suitable design resource, with sufficient range to make a significant contribution to small workshops, might be a series of publications containing design and build instructions for a variety of associated equipment, grouped according to either manufacture or use criteria. Since equipment is likely to be developed and tested on a piecemeal basis a system of individual publication as well as in compendium form may be the ideal, allowing specific designs to be obtained singly. If the compendium were in the form of a binder system the individual manuals could form the basis of the compendium, with later designs added.

If any external design input is to be made to rural workshops, it must be of the highest quality, well tested for shortcomings. This is particularly true in the case of designs of capital equipment for manufacture by primary workshops, since the number of copies produced will seriously magnify any design weaknesses. The dissemination of good design lessens the risk of dangerous or inadequate equipment being produced by less able local designer-producers; by the same token it places a great onus on the external agency to do the job properly. Failure to do so, besides harming the vulnerable immediate recipient, tarnishes the reputation of the system and therefore limits its future effectiveness. (The significance of the location of design and innovation activities is discussed later on.)

> The demand for threshers has led village blacksmiths and small town artisans in India's wheat bowl to produce their own backyard varieties, which find a ready market. These substandard machines are responsible for 50% of all thresher accidents, according to a study by Haryana Agricultural University. (Rao 1983)

As secondary workshops are concerned with repetitive output of whatever the product (or service) might be, there is considerable scope for external design input, since standardized production maximizes the exploitation of the input, which therefore justifies the effort of its manufacture.

Design related to the means of production can affect the entire output of the secondary workshops and can also be duplicated for use in any similar workshop. Where this involves capital equipment dissemination might be via the equipment fabrication manuals referred to above; such equipment would constitute design input to the secondary workshop by means of the primary. Likewise designs and manufacturing instructions for consumer items may also be assembled and published in groups according to manufacturing resource criteria.

For secondary workshops the value of jigs and similar aids to production is considerable, for as well as speeding up production they generally improve quality standards and the level of workmanship possible from a given level of skill. The greater the proportion of workers eligible for employment, the quicker the benefits of improvements in the local economy can reach all parts of the community. While there is a need to develop skills within the community, the de-skilling of tasks through the application of design accelerates the development process and minimizes problems because of a lack of skilled workers, as well as lowering the threshold above which on-the-job training can commence. Jigs usually relate to specific products, and so could form the part of the manufacturing instructions accompanying product designs.

If appropriate product designs and manufacturing instructions, including jigs, are being assembled and disseminated, the logical next step for the external application of design is to construct complete packages of product designs grouped according to the processes required for their production, together with designs and fabrication instructions for the capital equipment involved. Since manufacturing skills are not the only ingredient required for the success of a small workshop, some instructional material concerning entrepreneurial aspects of the business could also be incorporated. Each package would be product and market specific so the entrepreneurial material could be as precisely designed as the technology, including subjective costings to make it as brief and as relevant as possible. Requiring careful field testing to avoid any risk of economic or other damage to the recipient entrepreneurs or communities, such packages could be widely duplicated within a given context, fully justifying the level of effort taken to design them in the first place. However, any package would certainly require adaptation for use in different localities or contexts.

The entrepreneur 'in a vacuum' who is 'given' a ready made project by a small enterprise promotion agency, and does not have his own idea, must learn the technology if he is to have any hope of successfully converting the abstract project into a viable business; a skilled craftsman must similarly acquire some simple management skill before he can start and run his own business, but both technical and management skills can be acquired in many ways other than through training. (Harper 1984)

In the case of any technology which a development agency considers to be potentially appropriate within a developing country, whether the technology is innovative or suitable for transfer, it must first be carefully tested and applied individually, in order to be certain that the assumption of appropriateness is correct. Apart from the considerable inherent risks in employing technologies in a different context on a large scale without due preliminary research, there is, happily, not often going to be the opportunity to do so.

Since introduced technologies must be tested, and also demonstrated to the recipient countries and communities, they are generally tried out as part of a controlled project, or introduced in isolated test locations.

One of the problems facing the AT movement lies in its 'project' orientation. Pilot projects are very necessary for developing and testing prototypes, and for proving to potential users, producers, donors and governments that small-scale technologies exist and that they are technically feasible and economically viable. They are of little help, however, if the next step is not taken and if the technology fails to disseminate beyond the project boundaries. Successfully introducing an improved plough, mill, oil-press or water or sanitation system to a few villages, or introducing a new construction or industrial process to a few co-operatives or entrepreneurs is all very well. What is needed, however, is that such products and processes should be adopted, and come into use, in thousands, if not millions, of villages throughout the Third World. A handful is not enough, and at the moment, a handful of people is all that is benefitting in many of the examples cited. (Carr 1985)

A number of valuable contributions to small workshops in the form of designs for appropriate technology equipment already exist, most notably through the work of ApT for ITDG. However, experiences with this equipment illustrate the problems of dissemination. Distribution of construction manuals carries an inherent risk of low-quality manufacture, making the equipment dubiously useful and harming its reputation, and therefore its potential for natural dissemination. The alternative approach of having the equipment built commercially by a workshop in the

44

developing country, for normal market distribution at a cost much lower than the imported equivalent, is proving more successful, and has the advantage that, where a workshop still cannot afford this less-expensive item, the design, suitable for non-industrial fabrication, will nonetheless be in evidence in the country and can be copied. Actual equipment is more likely to be copied than published manuals, and does not require literacy on the part of the maker, in addition to which, unlike examples on demonstration tours, the commercially built item remains accessible for reference. Such a method of dissemination to the poorest workshops by means of the purchase of examples of the design by the better-off has definite attractions, and illustrates the value of such designs, even where they are to be built commercially, being suitable for non-industrial fabrication in small workshops.

The development of appropriate workshop technologies is not therefore the major problem, and can find some limited dissemination through commercial channels. While the need for such designs and equipment is perceived to be immense, it must be accepted that any natural percolation of the technologies will be exceedingly slow. It is accelerating the dissemination that presents the major challenge to interested governments and development agencies.

> Appropriate technologies can be (and have been) introduced and can be proved to be technically and economically viable, but their dissemination throughout a country or region will be severely limited unless the socio-economic climate is such that it will encourage both the manufacture and use of the new technologies. (Carr 1985)

The concept of the product-led package has obvious attractions, but the problems of dissemination will remain much the same once the package has been developed, even where the essential ingredient of compatibility with socio-economic and cultural contexts exists. The identification of an effective means of dissemination of appropriate technologies on a scale large enough to have a significant effect constitutes the major design problem in the development of rural industries. Avoiding astronomical costs and the employment of scarce government resources must be the ideal, but the scale of the problem and the varying environments within which it must be solved make an effective methodology elusive.

45

The development of dissemination techniques in order to identify a widely duplicatable solution and the assembly and organization of existing knowledge are the principal contributions that an external designer can make at the present time. While the need for the development of specific appropriate technologies does arise, these should be worked on as close as possible to the point(s) of application with the maximum involvement of all concerned. On these occasions external design professionals should restrict their roles as far as possible to that of informed catalysts. Such work should be carried out within specific projects, where the identification, or development, and application of appropriate solutions can be undertaken in context to ensure maximum user input and editorial control. At the same time the relevance and the contribution of such work to similar problems elsewhere should be continually examined.

The comparative viability of primary and secondary workshops

While the encouragement of primary workshops is essential to the blossoming of small enterprise, sufficient primary capability may already exist, as is the case in Zambia, if the use of it were common, and information regarding it were available.

Since capital, particularly foreign exchange, is limited it is important that it is deployed in the most profitable way for each workshop; in almost every case this would mean secondary workshop activity. However, for a rural manufacturer the available market may be too small to permit specialization, making primary manufacture and repair the only possibility, further restricting the possibility of competition with urban manufacturers. Concentration on secondary manufacture in this way would directly advance the productivity of the country's existing workshops, and for the individual would avoid the high capital and low productivity of a diversified primary shop. However, if all workshop owners confined themselves to secondary production the consequent lack of low-level capital equipment and of repair facilities would affect adversely any increase in the number of small businesses, which would be detrimental to small-scale industrial expansion as a whole, particularly in rural areas.

In spite of its awareness of the value of diverse primary

workshops, the Small Enterprise Promotion unit of the Development Bank of Zambia is reluctant to lend money to primary workshops since their diversity is unlikely to be profitable, a condition which is exacerbated by the difficulties in accurately monitoring costs on each different job (Schirra 1986). Since the essential requirement for any enterprise is to ensure that it be profitable, workshops should be encouraged as far as possible to concentrate on complementary lines which exploit to the maximum a minimum selection of capital equipment. One option is the manufacture of a number of carefully chosen products which, although all using the same processes, fall into two or three separate categories, each of which is aimed at a different market. In this way total dependence on a single market is avoided, but the time and energy required to market each item is kept to a minimum.

Categorization of small workshop production in developing countries

The principal categories of small workshop output are export goods, import substitution products, and products to meet basic or primary needs.

Export goods

The principal manufactured export goods of many developing countries are craft products. For example, according to a Lloyds Bank report (Lloyds Bank 1985) 16.2 per cent of India's exports of all kinds in 1983/84 were handicrafts, excluding the proportion of cotton goods, leather goods and jute manufactures which could be considered as craft-made. This compares with a 12.5 per cent share for crude oil, 7.0 per cent for engineering goods, and 5.1 per cent for tea, making handicrafts as a group India's most significant export. Of the country's defined manufactured exports in that year at least 40.1 per cent were handicrafts. This proportion was expected to rise as the government's recently introduced policy of ending subsidies for industrial cotton weaving and encouraging the hand-loom weavers took effect.

While export crafts can supply a significant amount of foreign exchange, they are frequently the product of those with other options for income generation, and may divert efforts from domestic production more relevant to development. The development of export crafts is justified in the

47

case of the disadvantaged, such as the handicapped, refugees or socially rejected groups. The principal trade-aid organizations in the UK all stipulate that the producer groups with which they deal should come within these categories and preferably be functioning as a co-operative (Pirie 1986). Since the annual turnover of Oxfam Trading, the largest of the UK agencies, was around £6 million in 1990, the contribution of this self-financing form of aid is significant, but it must be pointed out that in all cases the aid organizations' sales are dependent to a considerable extent upon the charitable appeal that accompanies the merchandise. There has been considerable debate within Oxfam regarding the role of its trading company, as to whether its primary role is to generate employment among the disadvantaged of the Third World, or simply to generate funds commercially for the parent organization to use in its development projects. This question has created internal disagreements affecting Oxfam Trading which are unlikely ever to be fully resolved (Ballyn 1986).

Many export-craft producer workshops require considerable back-up if they are to avoid collapse. In the case of hardship requiring aid this is acceptable, though ultimately undesirable, but in the case of small workshops which are intended to be commercial such a requirement is prohibitively expensive, and the shops therefore unrealistic.

While craft exports do bring foreign exchange into a developing country, they capitalize on cheap labour and existing technologies, with little effect on the development of the local resource base. Trade-aid organizations dealing with export goods invariably concentrate on craftwork; John Ballyn questions the validity of this (Ballyn 1986). If trade in less trivial products were encouraged the development of the manufacturing capability of small workshops would be enhanced.

In *Towards Village Industry* Krisno Nimpuno points out that:

> The producer seldom has any realistic ideas about the needs and wishes of his unknown customer. He will therefore have to produce mechanically and cannot design or adapt his products in a creative way to suit the needs of his far away client. It has been argued that UDCs should move away from import and export orientation towards an integrated domestic economy (Berg 1978).

48

As with agricultural cash crops, export crafts serve to reinforce the import/export economy, absorbing the time of the skilled makers who might otherwise constitute a basis for more relevant indigenous production. However, the purchase of central African traditional crafts on a large scale by Northern trade-aid organizations has been rare, because of a very poor reputation for quality control and delivery reliability (Lamont 1986), though the situation appears to be improving. John Pirie, of Oxfam Trading, makes the point that trading cannot be used constructively in the areas of greatest need, such as sub-Saharan Africa, since the people are generally not in a position to produce goods that are saleable in the developed world (Pirie 1986).

However, a virtue of the production and sale of handicrafts for external markets is that such markets are at a distance from local economic conditions, and therefore provide a source of income unaffected by them. There are, for example, about 162 women potters who try to sell their wares to tourists from a lay-by on the Beitbridge Road south of Masvingo in Zimbabwe. Their total stock is in the region of 15,000 pottery items, the quality of which is poor. Customers are few and sales are low, but in this area of very unreliable rainfall even this meagre income-generation opportunity constitutes an insurance in the face of frequent crop failure. If the pots were being sold within the community sales would cease when agriculture suffered, but the tourists are unaffected by slight variations in rainfall, making the production of pottery a lifebelt in the worst of times. (With the establishment of the National Handicraft Development and Marketing Centre in Harare there is greater potential for benefits from this production, but the realization of this will depend upon a significant improvement in product quality.)

Import substitution products
The manufactured products for which import substitution is sought in developing countries include luxury and consumer goods, the means of production and primary needs. Import substitution involves either the acquisition of the technology and raw materials with which to produce indigenously the previously imported product, or the local development of a substitute.

Where consumer fashion dictates that products should

have the appearance of being industrially produced, as a result of the cachet of the possession of imported goods, it is unlikely that such goods can be manufactured locally without the importation of the necessary technology, expertise and probably materials. This form of import substitution may be regarded as import replication. It is also unlikely that such manufacture is possible within the scale and resource of a small workshop. The price of the encouragement of consumer tastes according to the standards of industrialized countries thus extends beyond the diversion of resources from more development-oriented production to a perpetual foreign exchange requirement, and in the final analysis may not be cheaper than direct importation of the finished goods.

Where the means of producing a substitute product locally can be found, as opposed to substituting the manufacturing location of the same original product, the import requirement can be minimized and the development of local technological resources maximized; this form of substitution may be regarded as import replacement. Given that the indigenously developed product is unlikely to rely upon capital-intensive imported equipment, a far greater proportion of the income generated will pass into the hands of the local population.

While the substitution of imported luxury and consumer items with local equivalents is desirable as a means of reducing the requirement for foreign exchange, the development effect will be limited to any technological advance required for such manufacture.

Where import replacement is concerned with primary need the means of production or the benefit to development is potentially considerable, since every increase in local capability expands the national resource base. The expansion of the productive resource base, in its various forms, is of greater long-term development significance than the simple conservation of foreign exchange.

Products to meet basic or primary needs

The term basic, or primary, need indicates the priority which should be accorded to products which cater for it, for example, agricultural tools and implements, tools to make tools with, such as wood and metalworking tools, agricultural product processing equipment and basic domestic, health and educational requirements.

50

Primary need goods include those which may either be currently being imported or locally manufactured, as well as those which are unavailable either nationally or locally. The availability of an item from whatever source does not affect its status as a primary need good, although provision for a need that is unsatisfied should have a higher priority than the substitution of a primary need import.

The local manufacture of primary need products fulfils two development requirements. As well as providing the item which enables subsistence activity to take place it also represents an infrastructural resource base for the development of the community.

At the moment the priority is to produce simple industrial goods for agricultural or household consumption. It is possible to start the basic production of everyday consumer goods as substitutes for the present imports. Some of these goods can be made with the minimum of tools, skill and raw materials. (Berg 1978)

The greatest potential for a contribution to development lies in the manufacture of products to meet primary needs and equipment to expand the means of production, whether currently imported or not.

3. Relevance and Ignorance

The contribution of the small workshop

IF AGRICULTURE is the basis of the rural and national economy, and if agriculture is undertaken by people using labour-intensive methods, the provision, repair and development of appropriate equipment is essential. The existence of rural industry also provides employment when labour is not required on the land, increasing the viability of economic survival in rural areas and therefore countering the tendency towards rural depopulation and the economically damaging growth of urban conglomerations.

> If the technological levels in the rural and urban informal sectors are to be raised (as is, in fact, called for in the Programme of Action adopted by the ILO World Employment Conference), it is essential to adopt those technologies to which the small farmers, artisans and other small producers have easy access with their limited cash resources. This is not to suggest that modern technological know-how is not relevant or important, but only that a selective approach to the adaptation and adoption of known methods is needed. In fact, the experience of countries which have tried to implement a basic-needs strategy (eg China, Cuba, Tanzania) suggests that the improvement of simple village technologies is the only feasible approach to the gradual modernisation of the rural economy. The experience of Tanzania, which was examined in detail in an ILO/UNDP technical assistance project on appropriate technology, shows that in a subsistence economy the initial cash outlays required for imported equipment are far in excess of what the poor farmers can afford. It is therefore imperative to utilise local resources and skills for the design and development of technologies that are more productive than the traditional ones and yet are within the reach of farmers and other poverty groups. (Singer 1977)

The development of agriculture and of small rural industry are complementary. The improvement of agricultural efficiency depends upon its infrastructure, of which small industry is a part, while the development of such industry depends

52

upon the increase of agricultural prosperity to enable its products to be purchased locally.

For China, agriculture was not simply the production of crops but also the creation of rural industries integrated into the needs of rural people. The emphasis on rural industry is essential to the eradication of poverty in rural areas. (Berg 1978)

Whatever the initial level of local technology, the development of small workshops has the potential for a considerably greater effect than the simple provision of agricultural equipment. The generation of additional skills and the development of capability encourage innovation and the growth of manufacturing enterprises; the greater the proportion of a community's requirements that it produces itself, the greater the proportion of its income that is retained, which in turn encourages further growth.

Widespread rural industrial strategies can lead to the growth of new skills and therefore initiate the conditions for industrial change; precisely the conditions which foreign capital cannot create. Rural industrialisation would generate a widespread popular knowledge concerned with the material manipulation of the environment. The more industrially backward, which simply means the lower the level of technical skills, the greater the importance of all small industrial projects. Village industrialisation could create the atmosphere for manipulative technical knowledge which is so often lacking at present. (Berg 1978)

The economic and social importance of rural small-scale manufacturing is such that its development is now a major objective in many African nations, although the difference between understanding the importance of it and discovering the ways in which it can be best encouraged is proving a major problem.

Rural industries generate employment within the community, thus helping to minimize migration to the cities, either of the whole population or of individuals who then remit a proportion of their earnings to their family in the village. The availability of local employment maintains the social fabric of the community by providing a viable economic environment.

As well as the agricultural infrastructure and employment roles, small workshops also serve the community through the provision of other products which can improve the standard of living. The availability of domestic commodities, educational and health-related equipment and the tools and ancillary materials for building all permit the development of the resources and standard of living of the village.

The self-respect generated by small workshops, both for the workers and for the community as a whole, is significant, since pride in the resources and capability of the village encourages the energy necessary for further development. The example of a successful workshop also helps persuade other would-be entrepreneurs to take similar risks. 'Small enterprises are almost always locally owned and controlled, and they can strengthen rather than destroy the extended family and other social systems and cultural traditions that are perceived as valuable in their own right as well as symbols of national identity' (Harper 1984).

Just as rural industrialization is interdependent with the development of agriculture, so must it be socially appropriate to the community within which it exists. Large institutions are alien to a society based upon the extended family, and as such are liable to be a disruptive influence. To attempt to develop community agriculture or industry in a way that is not in harmony with traditional or existing social patterns threatens destabilization, since no change can be affected in isolation. '. . . appropriate technology or rural industrialisation has to be seen within a total socio/political strategy' (Berg 1978).

Though agriculture is the basis for national development in Africa, primary need exists wherever there are people. The population shift towards the large cities concentrates large numbers of people with little or no resources, for whom there is a minimum of employment or infrastructure. In an urban or semi-urban environment small workshops generate employment, while supplying products and services required by the community.

The activities of small workshops also generate income which is available for local development. In the absence of such subsistence resources as land or employment, it is only by the generation of self-employment that the urban poor can survive. Self-employment may mean the systematic scavenging of city waste dumps, as Mr Siziba pays boys to do in Lusaka, but this in turn may lead to the processing or use by small workshops of the scrap materials gathered.

It could be argued that the principal resource for the small urban workshop is scrap, such as tyres and metal. The production of shoes and other goods from tyres, of kerosene lamps, cooking utensils and charcoal stoves from old cans, for example, provides for the needs of the poor by the poor. The contribution of such recycling activities is significant in an economy where the majority of processed materials requires foreign exchange for their production or importation. Direct recycling, without further industrial processing of the material, is only possible in small workshops, where all operations are done individually, by hand. The production organization necessary in larger units does not permit such flexibility.

All small workshop activity develops the skills possessed by the people, which can be increasingly exploited as small industries are developed. The importance of self-reliance, both within communities and nationally, makes the growth of the small industry sector vital. Small workshops do not require substantial capital or technical expertise to set up and, within an African context, are frequently more productive and profitable for a given investment, as well as being more labour intensive than larger factories. 'The inherited colonial structure cannot be eliminated without an industrial strategy which aims at self-reliance instead of reinforcing the foreign ties, which would repeat present exploitations' (Tanzania 1973).

Whether a small workshop is rural or urban, the benefits accompanying employment for the people of the community are similar: self-respect, improvement of living standards through economic development and the provision of basic amenities through the enhanced capability of the community. In an urban or semi-urban environment, where migration has destabilized social relationships, the growth of infrastructure owned by members of the community themselves is a significant constructive influence.

The relevance of the small workshop within African development

While the scale of a small workshop makes its individual economic significance minimal, it is the cumulative effect of all the small workshops within a developing economy that justifies their energetic encouragement. The less developed a country, the more significant the proportion of its industry which is composed of small workshops is likely to be.

The scarcity of capital in developing countries is a major problem, affecting attempts to increase industrial production, at all levels. The capital necessary for a small workshop can frequently be raised from within the extended family, tapping resources which would otherwise remain unavailable for national development. Because overheads are minimal compared to a larger unit the capital requirement is further reduced. The majority of small workshops is labour-based, exploiting the skill of the workers and using a minimum of equipment; since labour is very cheap, while equipment, generally imported, is very expensive, a labour-intensive small shop is a more realistic proposition where capital is scarce. Labour-intensive small workshops are particularly suitable for the application of appropriate low-cost intermediate technologies, so the capital requirement can be further reduced by this means to a level which would be entirely unrealistic for a larger formal enterprise.

A general shortage of the management capability necessary to run larger businesses allows small workshops to compete on a more equal footing, provided that their management is sufficient for their level of operation. Nationally, the growth of the small workshop section of industry provides for the on-the-job training of managers, and the development of productive capability for a minimal investment and a minimal requirement for formally trained personnel.

Since the development of peasant agriculture is essential for the development of the majority of African countries, it follows that meeting the material needs of these farmers should have a high priority. If centralized industry, where it exists, or even imports cannot meet the needs of the peasant farmer because of the lack of a distribution system, then an alternative system of supply is an urgent matter. Goods produced locally by small workshops within the rural areas have little or no distribution problems, since they are made at or near the point of sale. The general existence of small rural workshops able to supply the equipment necessary for the requirements of local agricultural and related activities diminishes the significance of transport as a barrier to agricultural production and cuts out the cost of middlemen, a commercial distribution system involving considerable cost to the consumer.

If the desire for a materialist lifestyle is one of the attractions of the cities, however unlikely it is to be realized, the local production of domestic and consumer goods can go some way towards its satisfaction. While this does not satisfy the taste for imported goods, and cannot supply the more technologically based items such as radios and watches, local workshops could produce many domestic and income-generation requirements, increasing their availability and lessening the export of agriculturally earned cash to pay for them. In turn the partial realization of consumer expectations may help to retain in the rural population those, particularly the young, who may be tempted to migrate to the cities. Small rural workshops providing for local needs keep resources within the local community, since agriculturally earned income paid to the small workshop may then be spent again within the community by the artisan.

If workshops begin to develop and flourish, the gradual increase in rural production capability will produce a corresponding increase in local technology skill levels, allowing the exploitation of increased local prosperity by means of further agricultural development involving more developed technologies. If this increased income continues to be spent within the community, rather than outside it, the cycle of increasing prosperity and local development can continue.

The less the leakage of income to external suppliers, the greater the population that can be supported. In the overwhelming majority of cases, both nationally, in Africa, and between the global North and South, agricultural products and other raw materials tend to be priced down while manufactured and processed goods tend to be priced up. The resulting inequality of exchange ensures that suppliers of agricultural and other raw materials remain economically disadvantaged, in comparison to those who purchase them for processing purposes, and are therefore in a weak position when buying manufactured items from the economically more powerful. It follows that the more the dependence on outside sources for manufactured products can be minimized, the less effect the inequality of exchange will have. This applies equally between the economies of developed and developing nations and between rural and urban economies within individual countries. While rural/urban inequalities exist in virtually all national economies, the effects are particularly severe among the less developed countries.

Where urban migration has already taken place, the peasant influx constitutes a large population with few urban or industrial skills, for whom the cities have little to offer. Just as small workshops are a possible means of income generation in the village, so the same is true for the urban poor, with all the advantages of a far larger potential market and a plentiful supply of the commonest category of African raw material, scrap. The principal market for the majority of the informal-sector small workshops is the community of which they themselves form a part. All the advantages of low capital requirement for small enterprises hold as true for the urban enterprise as for the rural, offering an avenue of survival to the urbanized peasant. An Oxfam-supported aluminium foundry in Kinshasa, making dessert spoons from scrap using an imported cast-iron mould, supports two young men and two boys, giving them something like four to five times the income they could hope to receive in a factory. Their daily production of up to 700 spoons is sold direct to the customers at a price of 5 zaires (5 pence) each; the demand is so great that the entire output is sold from the workshop door. It is estimated that unemployment in Kinshasa is around 50 per cent, not including those involved in small-scale informal enterprises (Sier 1986). In such a context the ability to do something, to make something which others will pay for, is fundamental to survival. In a large population of unskilled unemployed, labour is cheap, but because of the cost of imports and the shortcomings of the national industrial base, consumer goods are expensive. The ability to produce such goods can therefore elevate the artisan concerned from the penury of the unskilled; development of the business through the demand for its product involves the training of others, enlarging the skill base, a vital resource for local and national development.

The supposition that in the face of shortcomings of all descriptions development can be achieved by general large-scale means involving a high level of technology has been clearly disproved in recent years. In spite of this, large schemes are still conceived and carried out. Developed nations giving aid which is 'tied' require that such money be spent in the donor country, usually on technologically advanced industrial products, since this has a beneficial effect on employment and industrial profitability, which are desirable political commodities on the domestic scene. Grandiose government-sponsored bureaucracies in developed countries appear incapable of supporting development projects which are other than grandiose, and are so far removed from the realities, particularly in the rural South, that their perception of the effect of their actions is severely limited. While the overall scale of the problems is immense the inability of such bodies as the World Bank to finance small-scale projects predisposes them towards the large scale; given the delicacy of equilibrium inherent in all the constituent systems of developing countries, large-scale projects controlled by executives remote from the point of application are potentially extremely harmful to those whom they are designed to help. The officials of developing countries are also prone to seduction by the prestige represented by major schemes. Where corruption is a temptation, the opportunities afforded by multi-million dollar schemes are infinitely greater than those inherent in a rural small-workshop development project.

In 1986 the Canadian government had recently reached an agreement with Zambia to refurbish and replace as necessary all heavy road-building equipment. The cost of a new starter-motor for a grader, or a similar piece of equipment, is roughly equivalent to the cost of 80km of hand-built road. The loss of income for the rural people who would have built the road by hand is catastrophic, but, worse, when the machines have again become useless in several years time the belief that roads can only be built by machine will have become firmly fixed (Gibson 1986). It may be that the inability of the bureaucratic mind in both Canada and Zambia to conceive of a good road being built about machines is one of the major barriers to rational and appropriate development. The same minds are likely to find it equally difficult to appreciate the potential and productivity of small workshops, since all their personal material requirements arrive painlessly, the product of capital-intensive industries.

The actions and decisions which promote economic development must come from within the country concerned if they are to be successful, whether or not some external assistance is made use of. In order to be successful such actions must be modest in immediate scale but as wide as possible in their application. One small workshop can equip another, and can also equip bigger ones; large industries are unlikely to devote energy to developing small competitors.

The failure of interventions

As the unemployment crisis in Africa has grown, fuelled by recession and the rising population, so governments and non-governmental organizations (NGOs) have increasingly attempted to address the problem. While unemployment in metropolitan and urban areas is uniformly high, it is partly the lack of opportunities for income generation in the rural areas which has generated urban migration, thus relocating the poverty. If jobs and non-agricultural income can be generated in the rural areas the pressure on the cities would be considerably less. Recognition of the inability of the formal sector to create sufficient employment in a worsening situation (Van Rensburg 1980:6) has led to a realization of the significance of the small-scale and informal industrial sector, which in turn has generated a growing number of interventions aimed at stimulating such enterprises. However, the success of interventions intended to develop rural manufacturing enterprise in central Africa is limited compared to their cost. Certainly there has been no widespread increase in productivity or generated income among rural enterprises.

There is no basis for assuming that rural manufacturing is being increasingly marginalized or is dying out, since in certain countries there is evidence of artisans choosing to return to their village from an urban area, for a combination of economic, family and quality-of-life reasons. The frequency of this appears to increase according to the growing poverty of the country concerned. However, there has been no significant improvement in the viability of their activities as a result of the many interventions which have been initiated, although such an improvement is needed desperately.

If there has been minimal success in the development of rural manufacturing industries in spite of widespread intervention this must be because either rural industry is inherently unviable in the context of the modern world or there has been a recurrent fault in the interventions.

> Many small rural industry programmes fail to integrate into the rural conditions. There are many examples of rural small industry projects, for which the raw material comes from elsewhere, and which are producing goods that are of little use in the village and will have to be marketed elsewhere. Such types of small industry obviously become very vulnerable in a village economy because of their dependence on outside markets and supply. (Berg 1978:8)

While an enterprise established on the basis described by Berg is unquestionably vulnerable, the integration of a business into rural conditions involves compatibility on a far wider basis than this would suggest. The expansion of rural manufacturing industry constitutes a genuine possibility under certain conditions, but the manner of current interventions is, broadly, faulty and is unlikely to have the desired effect; it may in fact be counter-productive.

Externally originating actions which have failed to produce the intended benefits may take various forms, but all have in common a failure to identify the true needs, both short and long term, of the consumers and/or the entrepreneurs serving them.

One of the most common failures is that projects are designed so that real or perceived dependence upon the external agents is an inevitable part of the package. Even where an intervention does not initially contain the seeds of dependence the inherently directive nature of the culture of the implementing personnel frequently influences the client-agent relationship towards dependence. In this regard expatriate personnel are particularly prone to a belief in the superiority of their own knowledge and experience, and are ill-equipped to recognize the value of existing local skills and knowledge. The same frequently holds true for development workers within their own country, since Northern-style training and qualification-consciousness generates traits associated with the acquired values. The arrogance of expatriate workers is frequently encouraged and confirmed by inverted racist attitudes on the part of recipient agencies and communities, interpreting the colour of a person's skin as indicating the possession of wisdom. Such neo-colonial attitudes are highly detrimental to the development process, since it discourages the expatriate from questioning and the indigenous person from recognizing the validity of each one's own knowledge (Katakwe 1986).

If a rural industry is to thrive it must be fundamentally sustainable. Any intervention which is likely to encourage dependency is by definition unsustainable and unlikely to achieve a positive result. If an intervention is to achieve a significant effect the results of it must be duplicateable. This requires that the inputs be compatible with the context, and must be of a nature and a scale which may be adopted by other interested entrepreneurs or communities without any

support from external actors. Given the scale of the requirement for non-agricultural income generation through rural
industrialization it is only by means of such autonomous
propagation that innovations originating internally or externally can have a significant effect. Any intervention which is
not specifically designed to these ends will fail, every failure
further confusing matters and making the chances of eventual success more remote.

While this caveat applies particularly to the activities of
expatriate agencies, it also applies to domestic agencies,
whether parastatal or NGOs; as long as their participation
remains an essential ingredient in rural industrialization the
extent of such development will continue to be negligible.
However appropriate their direct involvement may be in
other ways, their resources and size will always be far too
limited to have an effect on a significant scale. Only if they
are involved either in preparing the entrepreneurial environment, for example through political, social or fiscal measures, or in initiating appropriate innovation suitable for
subsequent adaptation and autonomous propagation can
such agents' activities result in growth on a significant scale.

The compartmentalization of the majority of external interventions into projects, neatly packaged for funding purposes, further promotes the tendency to see each
intervention in isolation and as an end in itself. If the design
horizon of each intervention is that of the initial project or
projects, no expectation of autonomous propagation is
aroused, and no consciousness of its importance as a goal for
each project is developed. Projects have a place, as the vehicle for the initial introduction of methods or means for
achieving the purpose of the project. But, as already argued,
unless the aim of the project has a much wider application
and can be independently adopted by would-be practitioners
its achievements will be insignificant and, by raising expectations and encouraging dependency, are likely to be counter-
productive in the longer term.

The confusion between qualifications and capabilities is a
common impediment to interventions concerning artisans. It
should be recognized that the perception of the decision-
makers is affected by the limitations of their own experience
and training. Thus a university-trained administrator within
an NGO will value similarly trained engineers with whom
s/he can communicate and identify, her or his self-

importance dictating respect for his peers rather than for, perhaps, an artisan. Thus the Zambian SIDO employs graduate engineers who have never worked at a bench to advise practising metalworkers on production methods. As a result, when Mr Mulenga, whose light metalwork fabrication business Mesco Products Ltd is located in the SIDO compound at Kitwe, requested assistance in the design of appropriate jigs, he was sent an engineer adviser almost totally lacking in practical experience (Mulenga 1986). The misapprehension that formal education equates with training ability exacerbates this. For instance, regulations in Malawi concerning the qualifications necessary for employment at a training institution meant that it was not possible for the Youth Rural Trades School at Salima to recruit an experienced blacksmith for a programme concerned with the training of rural smiths. Instead a metalwork instructor had to be recruited, to whom rudimentary smithing techniques were then taught (ITDG 1986). The inappropriate weighting of particular attributes or qualifications over others imposes a difference between the perceptions and experiences of the instructor or agent and those whom she or he is intended to assist.

Almost all interventions contain a difference in perception and experience between the agent and the recipient. If this is not entirely to negate the intervention it must be recognized and minimized. More than this, it must be acknowledged that the perceptions and experience of the practitioner are more directly valid in relation to her or his context than those of any external agent no matter how well qualified, since they are dictated by the environment in which the enterprise will subsequently exist. Even where the practitioner's perception and experience may lead to questionable conclusions, this constitutes the starting point of any development of their capability. Northern expatriates appear to experience particular difficulty in genuinely respecting the knowledge of those with a different background. One Norwegian volunteer, an ex-headmaster, working as an 'appropriate technologist' in Kitwe, Zambia, in 1986, designed a full set of European-style gardening tools which he then made out of locally available light scrap metal (Torp 1986). He was unaware of the inappropriateness of his endless energetic village lectures and demonstrations, which required the use of an expensive vehicle, and was at a loss to explain the almost total lack of take-up of the solutions which he was offering. His failure to recognize the worth and appropriateness of the traditional tools already in use prevented his perception of his own need to substitute tools which were normal to him for those that are normal in Africa. While this volunteer did no good at considerable expense, he also further handicapped any eventual development of appropriate technologies from within the villages themselves by encouraging a healthy disrespect for change, having characterized it as ill-founded (Von Krogh 1986).

To avoid such situations it is important that only skilled intervention agents with a flexible attitude towards their speciality, whose perceptions and training permit them to act as a catalytic resource to the indigenous subjects of intervention, should be employed. However, the level of expertise and understanding of a high proportion of intervention agents, particularly expatriate ones, is questionable, damaging severely the credibility of development agencies. Professionalism among agencies varies enormously, but in many cases inadequate consideration is given to the problems the activities are intended to address. The expatriate volunteer system is an obvious target for accusations of amateurism, varying enormously in quality and approach as it does among the various donor nations, but there is nothing to indicate that, given these differences, the quality of input is significantly lower among volunteers of a particular nation than among its professional development workers.

The most common form of incompatible and unduplicable intervention intended to further rural industrialization is the introduction, particularly of a training workshop conforming to the Northern pattern, equipped with electrically powered plant and tools. In a metal workshop these might include a lathe, a pedestal drill and a welding machine, while in a wood workshop there might be a circular saw, a band saw, a planer and a lathe. Several aspects of such an intervention are immediately questionable. The limited market in a rural area is unlikely to sustain such a workshop, making it dependent upon continued external support. It is also unlikely that the capital would be available locally to duplicate such an installation. Those trained in such a workshop will not be fitted for local employment in the absence of similar workshops, and will probably migrate to an urban area. Where such a workshop produces commercially, its impact on the local market is likely to be enormous, either driving existing practitioners out of business or restricting their market opportunities to the lower end of the quality and price scale, so lessening local employment opportunities rather than enhancing them according to their declared intention. A workshop in this form will condition local decision-makers and all those trained there to believe that this is what a workshop should or must be; anything else is an inadequate compromise, backward and unviable.

Liv Berg refers to the Kisarawe Street Project in Dar es Salaam which, although an urban workshop, illustrates many of these points: 'There is almost no use made of common facilities by the metal workers, since the machines supplied free from India proved to be of wrong type' (Livingstone 1978). Berg catalogues the problems, which include broken machinery which relies for its repair upon expatriate skills temporarily available locally; under-use of machinery; and inadequate training of artisans in the equipment's operation. In terms of the development of the capability of local artisans: '92.5% of the artisans declared that they had learned nothing from the management of NSIC (the implementing agency). No-one claimed to have learned "quite a lot"' (Berg 1978:43).

Training workshops established by Roman Catholic missionaries at Driefontein, Mvuma, Zimbabwe (wood and metal) and at Kikwit, Zaire (metal) share similar problems. Both have excellently established conventional workshops, with a high quality of training carried out by local instructors, graduates of the courses, under the guidance of expatriate technicians. In the case of the Institute Technique Professionel de Kikwit a very large workshop is equipped with 12 lathes (3 inoperative), 5 shapers (3 inoperative), 2 unused nibblers, bench shears, 3 drill presses, 3 milling machines (1 inoperative) and about 50 bench vices. The inoperative machines were largely the result of vandalism by the students, the lack of identification suggested by this causing the instructor considerable concern (Jacob 1986). There is no other workshop offering employment in Kikwit equipped with machinery of a similar level; the town's electricity supply is unreliable, and would make the profitable use of such equipment unlikely. During this researcher's stay in the area, when the training of others by the blacksmiths of Manie had begun, a graduate of the Kikwit course applied via the researcher to be trained at Manie. Although there was no smithing component in the Kikwit course he had attempted to teach himself how to forge, since he felt that there was no application of what he had learned there without migrating, which he had previously had to do, and working in Kinshasa. Of his three years at the Institute, two had been spent learning to use machine tools (Mudikosi 1988).

In other cases the establishment of manufacturing forms a component of a project with another specific purpose in mind. Oxfam supported a series of ox-traction schemes in the Kasai, in Zaire, which include the manufacture of ox-traction equipment. Much about these projects was excellent. However, each associated central manufacturing unit was established with a set of equipment imported from the UK at a 1986 cost of about £600 plus £300 shipping (Taylor 1986). No attempt had been made to find a way to equip the workshops from local sources or to relate the style of working to that in local use, which would have increased the possibility of their being imitated. At each of the workshops there are UK-manufactured forge tools which have not been used, since the training of the smiths has not covered these techniques. Such tools constitute a radical departure from local traditional practices, so the degree of duplicability is questionable. In the Project Rural workshop at Mbuji-Mayi, for example, the quality of the work was very poor, and would clearly not have been viable without subsidy.

The most remarkable of the Oxfam ox-traction workshops in Zaire was at Project Nkata, Mazuika, where a Belgian volunteer blacksmith had worked for ten years under impressively committed local project leadership. In a well-equipped replica of a European forge he had successfully taught the workshop staff to make European-style wooden cart-wheels, only to be frustrated by local consumer tastes for less suitable wheels made from more prestigious materials. Furthermore, the manufacture of some components was being sub-contracted to local traditional smiths. The project had provided the traditional smiths with London-pattern anvils, and had given them some training to ensure work of the necessary quality. However, the degree to which the project was dependent upon its centralized workshop and the expatriate volunteer suggested that insufficient thought had been given to the long-term future of manufacture and repair. It was clear that

66

manufacture was seen as incidental rather than central to the whole project (Taylor 1986).

There are many instances where the need to have particular services or facilities available for a particular project leads to the establishment of workshops which cannot be duplicated, and which appear to demonstrate that this is the only way in which the products can be manufactured. The conditioning of communities to a narrow Northern view of what constitutes a viable manufacturing enterprise is negative; each component of any project should be considered carefully in the light of its long-term effect. The organization of narrow projects with particular aims, by specialists, inevitably leads to complementary components, particularly technical ones, being treated superficially with unconsidered, and often unrecognized, side effects.

Perceptions of success

The most obvious indicator of the bias of Northern perceptions in business development area concerns assumptions of enterprise size. For example, the standard measure for small business used in Britain by the Council for Small Industries in Rural Areas (CoSIRA), now the Rural Development Commission, was that there should not be more than ten skilled workers. In certain exceptional cases this led to clients with up to 400 workers being eligible for the definition of small. Even by British standards such a definition places the limit well above a large number of businesses which produce a significant proportion of GDP, and which recently have come to be referred to as micro enterprises.

In the African context a business employing ten skilled men is likely to be well into the formal sector and to be modelled on Northern patterns. In terms of rural manufacturing enterprises such a scale is unusual and, where it exists, is likely to be externally owned. The vast majority of rural manufacturing enterprises are single artisan activities, at the most employing a handful of assistants. Where groups of producers work together, as the smiths at Manie, Zaire, or at Phalula, Malawi, they cannot be regarded as one business but as several 'cells' working in unison, possibly on an informal co-operative basis. In each cell there are unlikely to be more than four people, including the boys working as assistants to pump the bellows, in the case of smithing. Even in

67

cell groups of this size the nature of employment is frequently not according to the conventional Northern waged pattern, but may involve unpaid apprenticeships and extended family economic exchanges.

In addition to the tendency to single (or very few) worker enterprises the fixed and working capital of such businesses is far less than would be experienced in the North, even when compared as a proportion of the cost of labour.

It may appear pedantic to suggest that the much smaller scale of rural enterprises in Africa compared to the North is an important factor in the development interventions to which they are subjected. However, the judgement of what scale of business is worth supporting is crucial, since the distribution and nature of rural enterprises is a reflection of the social structure of which they form a part.

Where the social pattern of non-agricultural work has been informal, with activity taking place in or around the village, the centralization of activity through encouragement or inducements on the part of an external agent disturbs this pattern. For example, where production becomes centralized in a particular village those previously involved in the activity elsewhere in the area either become marginalized economically or begin a regime of travelling to work at the central location. 'Centralized' still applies as a description even where only a few kilometres' walk is involved. This immediately removes the worker from participation in family communication for a large proportion of the active day. For example, in Manie, Zaire, the blacksmiths normally work near or next to their own huts, so their contribution to the family group is continuous. This is particularly significant in regard to the supervision of children since if the men go out to work the whole burden rests on the women who are already under considerable strain), and to participation in village decision-making. Economic activity and travel outside the village greatly encourages the diversion of the cash generated away from domestic needs, thus further accelerating the social change likely to result.

The Northern concept of a viable workshop involves a designated building, properly built by Northern standards. Breeze-block walls and tin roofs create an initial capital cost far in excess of that which an indigenous rural workshop would ever be likely to meet (except through external loans). Such a workshop needs to broaden its market in order to be able to justify and cope with its high capital cost, which normally means a higher level of technology, for example welding, leading in turn to a still higher level of capitalization. A seasonal market is inadequate to sustain such an enterprise, yet the rural market is largely post-harvest in the early dry season, even where some access to work from large-scale farming is possible. Apart from the marginalization of other producers, for example of blacksmiths by the advent of welders, the social change and the capital debt incurred by the community, such a workshop requires industrially manufactured consumables which, when available, constitute a demand upon the village's cash earnings. Although the workshop's income may be far higher than that of a more traditional rural enterprise the amount of cash flowing out of the community for consumables and debt repayment will be far higher. If the activities of the workshop significantly improve the earning capacity of the community it serves, and which bears its costs, then such outgoings can be justified; if community earnings do not improve commensurately the apparently constructive workshop will become a drain on the community's cash resources. It is also likely to have succeeded in changing the communal view of what is required to manufacture and repair basic needs consumer items and agricultural equipment.

An example of this can be seen beside the market place at Mpika *boma* (village centre), in Zambia. A compound containing a metalworking shop and a carpenters' workshop was built by missionaries in 1973. Subsequently the complex was passed to 'The Self-Help Co-operative', formed for the purpose within the community. Visited in 1986 the enterprise was continuing to try to follow the training-by-production approach of the donors, with a full-time instructor employed for each discipline, both graduates of the workshops' three-year training programmes. Furniture-making was continuing, products being reasonable in spite of poor work practices such as cutting sawn timber to length with a bush saw. Workshop cleanliness and safety were poor. The metal workshop was effectively inactive. There were no welding rods, the pedestal drill was inoperative as a result of a motor burning out for the second time in a year, while the vice was drilled to bits and the anvil was totally deformed by weldspatter from use as a welding table. The only remaining hacksaw blade was brightly burnished with just one third of its teeth remaining. Not surprisingly, there was currently only one metalwork trainee, of whom there was no sign, while it was necessary to make two appointments before it was possible to meet the metalwork instructor, Mr Mulenga. The manager, Mr Mwansa, was absent on both occasions. While the workshops were continuing to exist they were dependent entirely upon both the income generated from their local clients and a further subsidy by the community. Their principal product, furniture, made no difference to the productivity of the community, while their greatest potential contribution, via metalwork and welding, remained unfulfilled because of the lack of consumables and expertise. Even had these ingredients been present there is a limit to the extent to which the client community possesses sufficient earning power to sustain such a workshop in appropriate productivity, even though the need exists.

By contrast, a traditional blacksmith working in the village was making a considerable contribution to the productivity of the community, particularly agricultural, through his production of axes, adzes, hoes and carving tools. Forty-seven-year-old Mr Kabuswe also made drums and wove mats. All these activities were concentrated in the dry season, since most of the rest of his time was taken up with farming. The capital level this one-man enterprise required was perfectly in proportion to its market and the resources of its clients. The concentration of his manufacturing activities during the dry season coincided with the short post-harvest period when his subsistence-farming clientèle had disposable income for the renewal of their tools and such-like. His principal constraint was raw material, requiring clients to bring their own scrap metal for him to work, which restricted the resulting profits.

The tendency to judge effectiveness according to size is common and, as suggested above, is particularly inappropriate in a seasonal economy. In many cases those involved in the development of rural industry are ignorant of the existence of part-time blacksmiths like Mr Kabuswe, and firmly declare that traditional blacksmithing has effectively died out, as Jens Muller describes (Muller 1980:123), but he goes further to suggest that another explanation could be 'lack of interest to bother about "backward" craftsmen'.

At present there is no worthwhile village/small scale industry which can undertake manufacture of hand tools and manually operated machinery in appreciable numbers. Due to the conspicuous absence of the traditional artisans and basic workshop tools, with the existing skills and resources, only very limited quantities of crude hand tools of poor quality can be manufactured. (Rao 1975)

Such ignorance and such attitudes are widespread among those involved in development throughout central and southern Africa. A formal resources survey of Luapula Province, Zambia, in 1987 declared that there were 72 metalworkers in the whole province. A superficial examination of the *status quo* in 1988 identified a total of 57 informal-sector metalworkshops, 45 being smithies, 24 of which were being visited by the author. Taken the length and breadth of the province in only four days, this sample was perforce concentrated near the main roads, where competition from urban manufacture and distribution was likely to be greatest. The smiths visited were discovered by choosing a pedestrian carrying an axe and asking where it was purchased. Doing this, in no case was it necessary to travel further than a kilometre from the point of contact in order to visit the maker, while in many cases it was a matter only of a few hundred metres (Poston 1988). The impression was of a startling density of part-time smiths. The same general pattern appears to exist in Tanzania, according to Muller, and in rural Zimbabwe in the communal and resettlement areas (Harries 1989), while in Zaire there are substantial tribal smithing groups at intervals across the country, the inheritors of degraded ancestral smithing traditions (Poston, 1988). Other evidence points to this being the case in most sub-Saharan countries.

Nonetheless, the small contribution of individual smiths, as opposed to the contribution of this group of producers as a whole, leads them to be generally ignored. Where notice is taken of them the tendency is to translate their activity into a more formalized Northern version of smithing, requiring more capital and greater output to justify it. In Malawi, an engineer proposing a training course for existing practitioners was adamant that it was only worth working with full-time smiths, because of the limited production of the part-timers. With one stroke a group of producers of enormous significance to subsistence agriculture activities was rejected in favour of full-timers more conventional to the Northern eye. For such full-time activity to be viable it must be located in a market town, where greater purchasing power can

71

sustain it and extend the season, thus removing the service and the income it generates from the rural area where it is most needed. The same project involved the introduction of locally made equipment which, while effective and well appreciated by the participating smiths to whom it was given, has never been duplicated by other smiths because the cost was out of all proportion to the earning power of the activity (ITDG 1988). The subsequent exercise in Malawi has successfully trained thirty part-time practitioners, most of whom have continued to practice their enhanced skills within their communities. The problems of higher capital requirements remain, though the adaptation of relevant technology from elsewhere in the developing world has considerably reduced this. One factor which discourages development work with rural part-time artisans who work within their communities is the fact that they are widely scattered and unrecorded and therefore require energy and commitment to identify and work with. This, coupled with their low profile, may suit the perception of the development worker and allow the justification of working in more centralized, convenient, and apparently productive locations.

Even where a successful full-time workshop has been established, it may remain under threat from well-intentioned influence and assistance. Mr Mazambani, formerly a grocer, had been retrained as a blacksmith as part of the pilot work for the project described above. Although the quality of his products was not exceptional, sharing with most others a shortcoming in hardening and tempering, he had developed his business within one year to the point where all debts were paid, he was employing four men and was handling regular orders for substantial quantities of tools from his workshop in the market town of Dedza. Quality was rapidly improving, with occasional visits and advice from the agency concerned, and he was expanding his product line spontaneously to include such products as metal shears and pick-axes, which he had worked out for himself how to make. A well-intentioned but unco-ordinated initiative by another agency then persuaded Mr Mazambani to take on a loan, with which he purchased an arc welder, an angle grinder and another item of equipment. Examination of his books within a month of these purchases showed that this side of the business was turning over just enough to repay the loan, probably without paying his wages. Not only was the owner drawn off from the forge, but his assistants' activities there would be required to pay for his time, unless there should be a considerable increase in trade with the new tools. If any of the new equipment, being used in far from ideal conditions, should fail, the forge would have to carry the debt, possibly of the complete loan, bearing in mind that the repair of such equipment can pose major problems. It is therefore reasonable to argue that a well-meaning attempt to assist this workshop by means of the provision of credit, frequently cited as a major restraint, may yet lead to the demise of an energetic, useful and financially sound tool-making enterprise. Even if the business survives experience suggests that the new equipment will eventually dominate the business, due both to the prestige of modern equipment and the greater purchasing power of those who operate vehicles, the principal market for welding. This is likely to take place without knowledge on the part of Mr Mazambani regarding the comparative profitability of the two activities, for though he is exceptional in keeping books carefully, accurate costing is unlikely. The far-reaching effect of such a shift in the dominant activity of the business may therefore be that the rural population presently supplied with tools by him will have less access to his services, while the urban-penetration related motor vehicle trade will be better served. However, the agency which made this loan will certainly mark Mr Mazambani's case down as a successful intervention, provided his business survives long enough for the loan to be repaid.

A similar approach can be seen at the Green Market, Mutare in Zimbabwe, where a large group of metalworkers and other trades is working seven days a week servicing the needs of consumers from the surrounding rural areas as well as the town. Innovation is clearly in evidence, particularly through the presence of a number of items of home-made capital equipment. In order to assist these producers, the stated motive being to improve their circumstances and earnings, an agency has built a major modern workshop inside a fenced compound on the edge of the market. The initial activity has involved the introduction of an impressive project manager, Mr Chitsunge, a social organizer who has been instrumental in forming a group of artisans to advise the project. He has also organized the beginnings of a raw material supply service, to be run on an economically sound basis, which addresses the most urgent need of the artisans, although this was handicapped by an inappropriate initial purchase recommended by an external expert. However, the next phase of the project is the employment of a technician and the installation of the already-delivered capital equipment in the workshop, which includes a lathe, pedestal drill, welding machine, grinders and other items, gifts of a foreign donor agency. The technician is then expected to train the market artisans in this workshop, and to service their needs using the equipment. The lathe is particularly questionable. At the moment, none of the basic needs products being made by the artisans requires the use of a lathe, so if they are trained to use one it is either a waste of time or they will subsequently take a loan to purchase one and change the nature of their business. The existence of the lathe will encourage its use when solutions to process requirements are being devised by the technician, where otherwise solutions possible within the artisans' own resources could be developed.

The change of product due to the introduction of a new process may well enhance the income of the artisan concerned, though the debt incurred may also make him more vulnerable. Similarly the use of the lathe to produce low-cost capital equipment may also boost the income of the producers in the market, so the aim of the project is fulfilled through both uses. But it is arguable that the perception which has given rise to the project aims is limited, and is concerned with the wrong target group. If the aim is wrong then the measure of success is irrelevant, since achieving the target will not achieve the desired result.

If the purpose of development is to benefit the maximum number of people, particularly in those areas socially and economically most crucial to the country's overall development, then any intervention must first look to those areas and the needs of the groups involved. Assisting one artisan is expensive, and if it has little effect beyond his own raised income is likely to have cost more than the resulting rise in earnings will amount to in a lifetime. If rural development is the key to national economic development then the needs of the rural population must be the primary concern of development agents. The Green Market artisans currently make scotch carts, windows, doors, hoes, and other welded and fabricated goods, as well as tinsmiths' domestic products, carpentry and so on, and have sufficient demand for these (principally primary needs) goods for them to work seven days a week. The diversion of even a part of this production into other goods, too expensive or not basically required by rural consumers, limits their access to the goods which are needed. So, the training of practising artisans to work a lathe may weaken the product support to the rural population.

The purpose of providing improved technology and introducing new skills is to improve the service to the rural, principally subsistence-farming, population. One way this is brought about is through the direct improvement of the artisans' products and productivity, as is the intention at Green Market. But the benefits of this are limited to the consumers who use this one market. Wider benefit will arise only if the skills and knowledge diffuse further, both through artisans leaving the market and setting up elsewhere and through artisans who visit the market recognizing the advantages of what they have seen and translating it back to their own circumstances. But in the case of Green Market it is probable that artisans will become dependent to a certain degree upon the services of such equipment as the lathe, and will therefore need to retain access to this technical resource, which means staying in or near Green Market. In the same way the technology developed by the project at Green Market cannot be taken from there by other artisans and translated to their villages because it would be remote from the lathe necessary for maintenance and repair.

The inappropriateness of training artisans in a context different from that in which they will practice has already been raised. In the case of Green Market the usual geographical argument does not exist, since the artisans will be trained in a modern workshop just next door to their own. However, they could as easily be trained in their own workshops, improving their own conditions, without the cost of the workshop and without the expectations it gives rise to.

In the same way the development of technical solutions in the modern workshop rather than in the artisans' shops greatly increases the risk that the solutions will be inappropriate. This risk is greatly increased when the shop's resources so far exceed those of the artisans.

The Green Market project will probably be able to claim success in a few years time, pointing to how the income of the market's artisans has improved. No measurement of negative effects is planned, because the possibility of there being any has not been recognized. The question will remain, however, as to whether the project will have been a constructive step in the development of Zimbabwe.

It is possible to dismiss the significance of one project, particularly where the effects are debatable, but not only is the Green Market project likely to confirm the same assumptions and approach to other development agents, but, since it is intended as a pilot project, it is planned to have its success replicated at as many rural centres as possible.

The limited perceptions which require indicators of success to be tangible and as physically evident as possible are reinforced by the tendency for Northern-conditioned agents to recreate their own environment in Africa. Rural industrial development is too often measured in terms of buildings, machinery, loans repaid and immediate turnover, things donors and agents may point to. Projects are conceived around superficial producer benefits rather than targeted consumers' needs for products. Many projects which have been considered a success by the agents involved are failures in real terms.

4. Artisan-oriented Intervention

The recognition of indigenous technical knowledge

The Gourma of Upper Volta have a highly developed world view that incorporates specific concepts and perceptions on human beings, souls, God and destiny. The Gourma are a pragmatic people, and are prepared to be innovative: but new developments must be based on Gourma perceptions, not on foreign concepts, if they are to succeed. Development agents need to consult the people, and to understand their views and their culturally recognized categories of labour; programs should not include elements of risk or experimentation, as failure would encourage people to believe their destiny was against such activities.

Substantial and effective improvement in the material well-being of any group of people presupposes that their own perceived needs and desires as well as means of attaining such needs and desires be taken into consideration. Any development intervention by definition implies change in old ways of doing things, change in ways of thinking. It seems to be true that such change can only have lasting and psychologically satisfying results for the people concerned if it comes from within the culture itself. Anthropologists recognise that every culture is dynamic in that it is always in a process of change, always in a process of self-redefinition. Such change, though seemingly slow and difficult at times to recognise, involves various members meeting and resolving material and psychological innovations and constraints on their lives. (Swanson 1980)

THERE IS NO QUESTION that the interventions which have been made in the past with the purpose of developing small-scale rural manufacture have had recurrent faults. That the intervention agents have arrived from an alien context with misconceptions is understandable, but the recurrence of the same faults is unacceptable.

While there is a series of identifiable faults which recur in rural industrialization projects, it is possible to ascribe the failures to one common factor. Interventions, by definition, come from outside the community, often from outside the country, through the agency of outsiders. Not only are these agents normally of a different culture, but, with rare exceptions, their education, training and experience are different from those who are the subjects of their attention. It is these very differences which qualify the agents in the eyes of those who authorize them, coming from the same background, since economic power lies with Northern systems and alliances, partly as a result of the domination of the Northern donors in the development arena. The attitude which has prevailed, and generally continues to do so, is that knowledge gained through the Northern form of academically based training is superior to knowledge gained in any other manner. This conviction on the part of the intervening agents leads to assumptions, conscious and subconscious, that the recipients are less knowledgeable and less intelligent than they themselves.

This arrogance on the part of external agents leads them to confuse the ability of people to help themselves with the ability of people to think for themselves. The resource poor generally do not have access to the means to solve their problems, and thus appear incapable. Those with the resources assume that their possession of the resources is a result of their greater knowledge and capability, and therefore tend to a presumption that the recipients require their direction.

> At the root of the problem lies the fact that officials — agricultural extension staff, planners, research workers, 'experts' and others — depend on scientific knowledge to legitimize their superior status. They thus have a vested interest in devaluing Indigenous Technical Knowledge and in imposing a sense of dependence on the part of their rural clients. This suggests that change may only be brought about through an assault at the level of ideology, and through a reorientation of reward systems. (Howes 1980)

The development of particular forms of knowledge and skill is a response to the social, cultural and environmental pressures on the society concerned. The development of Northern forms of knowledge has depended upon wealth to provide the means, and has in turn created further wealth. Knowledge fluctuates in all societies according to the prevailing conditions, leading to the domination of particular types of knowledge at particular times.

The economic domination of the North has therefore led to an extended domination by Northern forms of academic and industrially based education, training and practice. Evolved specifically for the development and support of an industrial society, these forms fulfil that function. In the context of a developing country they will also serve the same purpose, supporting formal industrialization and the functioning of a modern state. However, the relevance of such a purpose depends not only upon the state's wish to become a modern industrial nation but also upon the realizable possibility of the formal industrial sector dominating and controlling its economy, as it does in the North.

Given colonial influences and the direction that national development has taken in most African countries until the present time, the attempted progress towards formal large-scale industrialization is likely to continue for the foreseeable future, and will continue to exert political and economic pressure upon the policy and decision makers. Northern training systems are reasonably appropriate to this process, and will therefore continue to be imitated and strengthened by those promoting it.

If formal industrialization was rapidly becoming the norm in developing countries these formal training systems would be appropriate, but this is not the case. In all the developing countries in Africa a substantial majority of the population lives in rural areas, dependent upon subsistence agriculture for its survival. Even in urban areas formal industry is increasingly unable to provide employment for the rapidly growing numbers of unemployed people. Northern knowledge systems, developed for Northern industrialization, only marginally relate to these people and their needs; the use or imposition of them in this context is therefore entirely inappropriate and counter-productive.

This does not mean that knowledge acquired through Northern systems is irrelevant to subsistence agriculture and rural communities, but rather that it must be offered as a resource alongside indigenous technical knowledge, to be used at the discretion of the community, rather than imposed as a replacement.

Respect for the poor and what they want offsets paternalism. The reversal this implies is that outsiders should start not with their own priorities but with those of the poor, although however much self-insight they have, outsiders will still project their own values and priorities. (Chambers 1983)

One basis upon which a culture may be judged to be evolving in a healthy way, with a minimum of cultural alienation and disorientation, with a minimum of breakdown in family solidarity and continuity, is the extent to which change is permitted to develop from within the culture itself. As long as change and change agents work from within particular cultures and existing frameworks of ideas, a culture may be said to have maintained its traditional nature — in spite of the fact that it may be evolving into a modern, self-determining society. Unfortunately such change is more often from the outside. Development programs are often designed upon the basis of foreign concepts which in the end either fail or become a form of ideological domination of various peoples. The consequences of disruptions in traditional authority lines, of the raising of new needs which may not be consistently met, of changes in the accepted division of labor and labor organisation, and new means of manipulating power and available resources may destroy the initial advantages an aid program in development might have. It has recently become popular to speak of involving target groups in the identification and solution of their own problems. Yet in practice, for lack of relevant sociological and anthropological data (which often results in the assumption that one already knows all one needs to know about a particular group or that the target group would not be capable of suggesting real solutions to their real problems), projects are still often set up without true consultation with the communities concerned, without understanding of the various constraints and incentives placed upon them by their culture and environment. (Swanson 1980)

In the context of rural manufacturing, therefore, all inputs should be oriented to the recipient society, particularly the consumers and artisans, and directed by them. While the agents' expertise may be extensive there is no way to guarantee its relevance and therefore its constructive nature. The external agents do not take the risks, and are not the victims in the case of failure. The knowledge and culture of the recipient community form the medium in which all development takes place; but since it is the survival of their society and they themselves that are at stake it is they who should control changes within that context. Therefore all developmental action must be informed by and start from the existing technological, social, cultural and economic situation. That this is not normally the case accounts for the rarity of success in the development of small-scale rural manufacturing.

80

Traditional cultures and value systems are to be respected rather than demolished. Development is not a matter of modern Western standards and attitudes bringing about the expected social change from traditional to modern society. Transfer of technology is not always beneficial. It can lead to social dualism and other forms of maldevelopment. (Dr Kinhide Mushakoji, Vice-Rector of the UN University's human and social development program, Moore 1979)

The control of interventions

It is only by means of artisan-oriented intervention that the possibility exists for the development of the artisans' innovative capacity and therefore their adaptability, an essential ingredient if their activity is to be sustained in the longer term.

By definition an intervention comes from outside the situation which it is intended to affect, and is therefore likely to be controlled by outside forces. In the context of development it is from the lack of power which exists at every level, from national to the poorest individual, that the need for assistance and development arises. The economic position of the less developed countries leaves them with little power to affect their own situation which, forming part of the world economy, is effectively controlled to their disadvantage by the Northern countries. The resource-poor individual similarly has little control over her or his situation, being subjugated to all the levels of power and authority within the country and, ultimately, to the external economic forces which control the national situation.

The fundamental control over interventions resides in the Northern countries, the donor nations. This is true in every sense, since trading and political interventions constitute even greater influences than donor interventions, but for the purpose of this argument the term 'intervention' will be taken to mean an intervention which is intended to have a beneficial developmental effect.

The individual, supposedly the ultimate beneficiary of any development, has no control over an intervention.

A local grouping, whether a village, an association, a co-operative or whatever, may be able to influence those who control an intervention in the best cases, but if their wishes do not coincide with the views of whoever is in control there is a risk that no intervention will take place. For people who

81

realize their own need for support and development the refusal of an intervention because the terms are not right is extremely difficult, on the basis that any help is better than none. The conviction that an intervention may actually be damaging is particularly difficult to sustain in the face of the insistent expert opinion of well-educated outsiders and foreigners, particularly when self-interest may affect the reasoning of some of those within the group. However, a group remains in a much stronger position than an individual, since those who control interventions cannot work with individuals and, by their nature, understand groups better. In certain cases one group may use this power against the interests of other individuals within their community.

The next level of participants in an intervention are formalized local organizations, institutions and functionaries. Local organizations may have a strong influence upon interventions, but are generally dependent upon external funding for their ability to act, and do not therefore have the ultimate control. While such organizations may be regarded as being close to those whom they wish to assist, keeping the control of the organization in the hands of the people it is intended to serve is extremely difficult and assumes altruism on the part of all of those who are involved, particularly in the management of the organization. There are examples of local groups retaining a high level of control, for example the Organisation of Rural Associations for Progress, based in Bulawayo, Zimbabwe, but this is achieved by a high level of exclusion of other agencies, since experience has taught that external participants seek to control (Hussey 1989).

Institution personnel normally see themselves as existing to benefit those whom they apparently serve. The principal institutional development activity is training, usually patterned upon a Northern model and therefore relating to the needs of a Northern industrial society. Within the confines of government policies, the institutions do possess an element of control over what is taught and how it is taught, and take their responsibility for directing this seriously. However, those working in institutions have a degree of insulation from the conditions which they wish to affect, and, being fully employed, are not in a position to maintain an intimacy with the conditions of those they train. When change is seen as desirable, institutions cannot by their nature adapt quickly and are likely to have a struggle to remain relevant to real needs. Institutions have a vested interest in their own existence, which severely limits their ability to recognize the limitations of their effectiveness, particularly in a context which is evolving rapidly. Thus the control which they do possess is liable to be a confining one, while remaining dependent upon external sources for funding, the ultimate control.

The functionaries of state or parastatal organizations may perform an editing function, but have little real control. The nature of their intervention is defined at higher levels, from where financial resources are controlled and to which they are responsible.

Control begins to exist above this level, whether in national government offices, in national or international NGOs or in expatriate donor agencies, charitable or statal. The source of money is where control ultimately lies, whether national or foreign. No funds are disbursed without some degree of accountability in the form of monitoring, which carries with it a directive element, influencing and controlling policy. The governments of developing countries and NGOs within those countries do have choices of where they try to obtain funding from, but this only varies the level and nature of controls. There is no source of funding without control.

As long as external funding is required to fuel an intervention it will not be controlled by members of the target group. However, accepting that control remains with the paymasters for as long as external funding is required, which means at least in the formative stages of the initiative, it is nonetheless possible for the responsibility for the direction of the intervention to reside with the target group to a major extent, and this should increase as the initiative progresses. In this way the control which continues to be exercised externally will only be that of a funding veto, rather than an ongoing control over content.

The practice of an agency measuring opinion, assessing it and acting accordingly is not the same as giving over the direction, but rather acknowledging the direction indicated. While this approach may appear to reach the immediate desired end, it fails to build up the group's ability to direct its own future, which is necessary if further development is to be carried out autonomously or with minimal external participation. Where the intention is for the responsibility for the direction of the intervention to reside with the target group,

83

the way to work with the most needy nonetheless remains elusive. It is difficult for the poorest people to organize themselves to work together to influence or direct an intervention, because of the extreme nature of their situation. Where some degree of organization is achieved it is frequently among those in a very slightly better position, though still falling well within what is considered to be the target group of the intervention. In such cases there is a serious risk that those poorer than the organized group will ultimately suffer losses as a result of the intervention. Within different social groups certain classes are better able to organize, are in positions of greater power, or form part of alliances based upon self-interest. The most general example of such groupings is gender, males retaining most of the control in the majority of societies, to the detriment of females.

In the same way as other interests will influence decisions, the national policy environment will always have a significant effect upon any intervention, controlling its existence, its immediate effects and the duration of them. All interventions within any country should be carried out, if not by the government itself, then with its knowledge, support and approval. While a government is a power grouping which can never represent the interests of all of the people, it remains the immediate controlling force within its territory, even if all governments are not moral and universally well-intentioned. In such cases there may be a conflict between the view of the government and that of the agency wishing to sponsor and undertake an intervention, at which point the ownership of control and its manipulation may be of great significance. Such situations are not infrequent, the only constant being that, whether the control is national or external, those who will be most affected will not have it.

The significance of the control of the paymasters, therefore, is that it includes the choice of who will represent the target group, who will be allowed to direct the form and content of an intervention. Given a willingness to divest the responsibility for the direction to such representatives, this choice remains crucial to the effects of the intervention, who are the winners and losers, and the extent to which the results will endure.

The lack of control of the poorest people over interventions made on their behalf means that such interventions are always at risk of being misconceived, misdirected and inappropriate. While there is a risk of this whoever controls the intervention, the further the control lies from the point of impact the less likely it is that the intervention will be appropriate. It is therefore necessary to invest as much of the direction of an intervention as possible in the hands of those nearest the point of impact. Who these people are will, inevitably, vary.

Respectful collaboration

Precisely because the normal approach to the development of small-scale rural manufacturing has not been oriented around the consumers and practitioners themselves it is difficult to illustrate the alternative approach proposed here. There are, however, a few examples, including one in which the technical development input was made under the direction of the recipients and emerged naturally out of the circumstances which arose. The possibilities and the direction in which the dialogue developed were clearly indicated by the people themselves recognizing and responding to their own situation and requirements.

The blacksmiths of Manie, Zaire

Manie is a village in the Zone of Bulungu, Bandundu Region, Zaire, with a population of about 650 people of the Bangongo tribe, who speak Kingongo, and is about 20 miles from the agricultural training centre of Lusekele. Two other nearby villages of the same tribe, Kingangu and Bangongo, also have a number of forges, but fewer than Manie's twelve. Besides the smiths Manie also has basket makers, potters and a carpenter. The surrounding country is open bush, agriculturally very poor. There is visible evidence of malnutrition among the children of the village, and a high mortality rate. The Bangongo are known to have been smiths for hundreds of years; there are examples of the work of their ancestors in the National Museum in Kinshasa.

The project arose out of a brief visit paid to Manie in December 1986 by the author and Gary Selig, Director of the Centre Agricole de Lusekele. The blacksmiths made it clear that their principal problems were the lack of smithing tools, particularly tongs, and raw materials. Asked why they did not make their own tools, the smiths replied that this was not possible, since such tools as tongs must be produced industrially. Although the smiths were asking for access to imported tools, most of the tools they needed could be made in the village forges, given the appropriate technical knowledge, while imported tools were forbiddingly expensive and were anyway largely unavailable even in Kinshasa. The introduction of the necessary techniques, which would be far more beneficial and have a longer-term effect than the supplying of a consignment of tools, was not suggested at this time, since there was no way of knowing whether the necessary finance could be found.

When the necessary funding had been made available by the Beatrice Laing Trust, a British charity, with accommodation, support and transport being provided by the Communauté Baptiste de Zaire Ouest (CBZO) mission at Vanga and the Centre Agricole at Lusekele, a proposal was sent via Gary Selig and the Lusekele Pastor, Tata Wanga, requesting that the author should be permitted to come from the UK to work with the smiths in the village. This visitor was definitely not to be a teacher, but a fellow artisan who would be willing to trade technical knowledge. This emphasized the respect of the visitor for the indigenous smiths, although it made the visit harder to explain and aroused suspicions that their traditional wisdom would be stolen.

These doubts were encouraged particularly by one older smith, Noël Mutapa, who later turned out to be the principal village sorcerer. There had previously been tension between the smiths of the area and the missionaries, since smithing is central to fetishism, and this had culminated in 1973 in over-zealous Zairie catechists persecuting the traditional smiths and driving them outside of a ten-mile radius of the mission. Noël saw the author as a spy for the missionaries, whose intention would be to discover fetishistic practices and recommence the persecution. Consensus opinion among the smiths and the support of the area Chef de Groupement overcame these doubts, so a message was sent back to say that the visit could take place, though Noël's feelings were only gradually mollified as the visit progressed. (The author's willingness to drink palm wine helped to convince the smiths that he was definitely not a Baptist missionary.)

On arrival in the area two meetings were held and, with the strong support of the Chef de Groupement, it was agreed that the visitor would work in a particular forge on a daily basis for a period of five weeks with whoever wished to work with him. The only tools which he brought into the village were two German-pattern forging hammers, two files, chalk and, in reserve, an oil stone, dividers and a rule. There was much heart-searching about the hammers, but since the Bangongo used only traditional unshafted pounding hammers the author was nervous of his ability to communicate techniques without a European-style hammer. There was no intention to change the type of hammer the smiths used, but this did in fact happen with some of the smiths who decided to experiment with the different type and now use either, according to what they are doing. Files are anyway purchased from Kinshasa by the smiths, so the motive was not to use up their resource, while chalk was intended as a means of communication.

The working relationship was highly successful, a group of about six blacksmiths choosing to work regularly with the visitor, while others were occasional participants and observers. Principal among the cadre was Waka Ngai, the master-smith who, directly or indirectly, had taught every other smith in the village. Communication was in French, a number of the younger smiths speaking it fluently; one in particular was invaluable as an interpreter. Working in two languages had a surprising benefit, since everything that was said would be repeated, giving all those with both languages a chance to examine their comprehension and discuss it. An unexpected initiative was the appointment by the cadre of a secretary, Manwanna, who proceeded to record notes on all technical matters throughout the visit.

The author worked only in the mornings, in order to minimize the disruption his presence would cause to normal commercial activity, both for the sake of the smiths' limited incomes and the supply of agricultural tools to the local population. In the event the smiths frequently continued to work on the tools that they were making after his departure each day, and astonished the Agriculture Centre staff by continuing such work over the weekend in order to show the result to the visitor on the Monday. This was considered to be completely out of character, and had, earlier, been considered an impossibility.

During the 20 days actually spent working together in the forge, the Manie smiths made the following new products, chosen and prioritized by them:

- o   Headed nails (and associated anvil tools)
- o   Rivets (and associated anvil tools)
- o   Drifts
- o   Punches
- o   Chisels
- o   Tongs
- o   Pincers ('tenailles')
- o   Hammer head (approx 1500gms)
- o   Pruning shears.

They also learned how to upset, anneal, harden and temper steel, and, through the agency of the visitor but from a smith at Bangongo, how to fire-weld, a traditional technique which had been lost to them. The ground covered was directed entirely by the smiths, the visitor's input to the curriculum being to arrange the order in which tools were introduced so as to make the progression logical.

There was much discussion regarding the relative desirability of reacquiring the knowledge of fire-welding either from the visitor or from within their own tribe, since discussion and enquiry had revealed that the knowledge had been retained in the neighbouring village of Bangongo, though it was now used only for making traditional hammers. With the visitor's full support it was decided that the smiths should try to reacquire the knowledge from their own people, since this would involve the retention of the customs and beliefs attached to the technique. This provided an opportunity to demonstrate the respect in which the visitor held traditional beliefs. The process also developed the working relationship, since the disclosure of the hidden significance within hammer-making, and therefore fire-welding, was a considerable display of trust in the visitor on the part of the smiths. The author, to his delight, was present when fire-welding was demonstrated to five of the Manie smiths by a member of their tribe in the next village on the last day of his stay.

A gunsmith from Kilusu, Thomas Ngangu, also became aware of the visitor's presence and participated in a number of the sessions at Manie, principally benefiting from learning how to temper the springs of his guns. Thomas requested permission from the Manie cadre to make his own copy of their technical notes, which was granted, and he then copied them out by hand. The smiths of Kingangu and Bangongo did not send delegates on the first visit. There was some

88

uncertainty as to whether they had received the invitation, or whether the question of which was the host village interfered with their participation, but ruffled feelings were largely calmed by the end of the visit.

As the collaboration progressed the question of how things might go forward, and how the wider community might benefit, were discussed. It was suggested that Manie might become a Technical Centre for the blacksmiths of the surrounding area, passing on the knowledge that they had gained. The smiths recognized that there would be no money from donors with which to build smart workshops or buy tools, but that the centre would consist of the knowledge of the smiths being made available to others. The smiths would instruct any blacksmith from elsewhere in the making of a particular tool for a fee, which was to be twice the selling price of the tool in question, the instructor keeping the tool made in the demonstration. This form of teaching transaction does bear some resemblance to the traditional systems and constituted a culturally acceptable response to the situation for the smiths. The benefits to the Manie smiths would be prestige, some income, and the expectation that they would be the first recipients of any future technical inputs, in recognition of their willingness to share their knowledge with other smiths. There was considerable enthusiasm on the part of the blacksmiths, to the extent of asking publicly for help to realize this scheme at the Open Day feast which was held to mark the end of the author's visit. Both Pastor Pambi, the region's senior pastor, and Gary Selig promised to commit their efforts to the idea.

The development of this idea, and the willingness of the smiths to undertake its implementation, was a remarkable departure from normal development experience with traditional smiths. Lars Ove Jonsson reports that even Jens Muller (Muller 1980) took three years to find one smith in Tanzania willing to share his knowledge with outsiders, the man in question being an old man whose sons were all dead (Jonsson 1986).

The author left Manie after five weeks. The length of time was appropriate, since while working with him the smiths were not earning their normal income, and the time was short enough for concentration and commitment to be maintained. As masters in their own right, what the smiths can learn in a short time is considerable; the techniques covered on this occasion were probably as many as could be assimilated easily at once. It was agreed between the smiths, the author and Gary Selig that, should it be possible, a further visit by the author would allow a Technical Centre to be set up. The author's presence was desirable since a considerable amount of travelling would be necessary to identify and visit all the practising blacksmiths within the proposed 20 to 30km radius of the village, with transport being provided by the mission. The smiths also felt that his support was desirable in other ways, not least because he represented an interest outside any potential tribal rivalry.

As a consequence of the success of the first five weeks, the author spent a further five weeks in the area during February and March 1988 in order to help establish a self-contained system for local technical transfer, at the invitation of the blacksmiths and the CBZO. Accommodation, support and transport were again provided by the Centre Agricole at Lusekele, a CBZO mission, while the project continued to be financed by the Beatrice Laing Trust.

Six months after the initial input almost all of the transferred knowledge had been retained and exploited. The cadre of Manie smiths was still eager to disseminate their new knowledge more widely among artisans of neighbouring tribes, a radical departure from normal local practice. Having therefore secured the formal approval of the blacksmiths of Manie, the author carried out a programme of visits to all the identifiable practising smiths within about 30km of Manie, between the rivers Kwilu and Gobari, accompanied by a delegate of the Manie cadre, Mafuta Mopati, who also acted as guide and interpreter. The response of all the blacksmiths visited, whether working in groups or in isolation, was overwhelmingly positive. Where smiths had been absent from their forges, this being the agriculturally demanding rainy season, they generally turned up at Manie within a few days in response to the information left with their families or neighbours. In addition to the enthusiasm of the blacksmiths the response of consumers to the sample tools which were carried was most encouraging.

Over seventy blacksmiths practising within the catchment area were identified and visited, including those of the Bangongo living in Manie, Bangongo and Kingangu. They included traditionally trained smiths and those who had received a formal technical training or an apprenticeship in metalwork or mechanics. A significant number had established their workshops comparatively recently, while there was frequent evidence of others wishing to do so.

Training by the Manie cadre began almost immediately, the visitor being careful to absent himself on the designated days, Mondays and Fridays. The first trainees were of the same Bangongo tribe as the Manie smiths, but arrangements for the training of those from other tribes was well in hand before the visitor's departure. The standing joke was that the Manie cadre was now prepared to teach absolutely anyone, even a *mundele* (a white man). Significantly the first tools made by those trained by the Manie smiths were generally of a standard similar to those made by the instructors themselves and were immediately usable. The trainee smiths appeared to find the instruction acceptable and beneficial, once some teething troubles and the greed of one instructor had been dealt with by the smiths themselves.

Further concentrations of blacksmiths in other areas were also identified, for example over sixty around Dué III, a village 100km from Manie, who indicated considerable interest in similar assistance. The potential and the demand for the duplication of the technical transfer system elsewhere appeared, and appears to be most promising. To this end Gary Selig did apply subsequently to relevant donor agencies to finance the appointment of a resident tutor-smith, for an initial period of two years, who would encourage the establishment of additional centres and further advance the existing pilot one, while training two local counterparts to continue the programme after his departure. Unfortunately it has not yet proved possible to obtain funds for this.

While it was not the intention to make additional technical input on the second visit, apart from any necessary consolidation of the previous contribution, some further work was done, more by stimulation than by workshop participation on the visitors' part. The most significant advance was the successful adoption of fire-welding as a technique; while it had been demonstrated to the Manie smiths by one of their kinsmen at the end of the previous visit, a lack of confidence had prevented serious experimentation. However, the proposal of its use for the hard-facing of hammers made of vehicle half-shaft steel with leaf-spring steel motivated an attempt which was resoundingly successful. The resulting boost to their confidence produced a new willingness to experiment with other products, and quality articles such as carpenters' hammers, and plane and spokeshave blades, began to appear. Various hammer forms quickly came to be regarded as routine products, with fire-welding being taken for granted.

In addition to the new confidence a significant increase in the quality of their workmanship occurred during the period of this second visit. As an experiment, two sets of letter stamps to spell the village name Manie had been brought out from England, as well as a small branding iron with the complete name on it, as a gift paid for by the congregation of St James' Church, Friern Barnet, London. These could have been made in the village, but constructive gifts to the whole group are not easy to identify. The purpose of the gift was to investigate the effect on the market of identifying the origin of a product, which is not local practice, and in this way to imitate some of the outward conventions of the industrially produced competition, and to bring the pride of the craftsmen into play in order to raise the quality of their output. The punches occasioned great excitement and amazement, tempered by the warning that while a good market tool would attract customers, a poor tool whose source could be identified would have a powerful opposite effect. For about three weeks the punches were not used, even on long-established product lines such as hoes; they were used first at the visitor's insistence that a hammer head he was buying should be marked. In the meantime the quality of all new products improved dramatically, the connection between quality, reputation, market and income having been clearly understood. Given the considerable poverty of the people and the consequently desperate need for cash, the most astonishing change in attitude was demonstrated when the prices which the Lusekele Centre would pay for hammers were being discussed; the visitor was told that the price received was currently seen as being of less importance than getting the product right.

In Manie the initiative was subsequently predominantly taken by the younger and more motivated smiths, particularly Mafuta, Makay and Mikibu. The inventiveness of their work clearly improved in line with their confidence, particularly during the period of the second visit.

There was at this time a great deal of discussion about commercial matters, particularly those concerning costing and working capital. The smiths were concerned about their vulnerability in these areas. Further progress was also made towards establishing an improved supply of raw materials through Lusekele, which was vital if the progress made was to be sustained (Poston 1989).

The situation at Manie was monitored by Gary Selig, until his departure on leave in early 1989. At that time he reported that the smiths were continuing to make the new tools and to sell them as products to the local community, including the agricultural centre's shop. It appears that they continued to teach the techniques to others when they were requested to do so. Sadly, Waka Ngai, the 'master of masters', died in 1989, probably poisoned by members of his own clan. In November 1990 products were still being made and sold to the agricultural centre, particularly by Makay, but Gary Selig was unable to visit the village before he finally left Zaire to continue his work in Brazil. Since that time there has been no information about production or training in Manie.

At all times the ownership of the dialogue and the technical transfer remained with the smiths, and the process was controlled by them. The relationship was not confused by hopes of material gifts, since only knowledge was on offer. The speed of advance and the level of input were always related directly to existing knowledge. Incremental technical transfer means that each acquisition of knowledge is assimilated into the smiths' own traditionally gained repertoire before the next input is received, so that the new knowledge never appears disproportionately large. Since confidence is the key to artisanal learning and development, this is a fundamentally important point.

The blacksmiths of Mtwara and Lindi regions, Tanzania

Since Manie the approach has been developed and adopted by ITDG in Malawi and Zimbabwe. The most recent and extensive use of it is being made by the SIDO offices of Lindi and Mtwara regions in Tanzania, funded and supported by the FINNIDA-sponsored Rural Integrated Project Support (RIPS) programme in partnership with ITDG, who have provided technical training inputs.

An indicative census of blacksmiths was carried out over three weeks in the two southern coastal regions of Tanzania, Lindi and Mtwara, something which had not been done before. Two large areas were excluded from the survey, and coverage overall was recognized as incomplete. Nonetheless, 630 blacksmiths were identified and interviewed in an area with a population of 1,536,044 (1988), which gives one blacksmith identified by the census per 2438 people. A good smith working full-time with access to steel can produce 100 *jembes* (hoes) in a month, so it is reasonable to suppose an average annual output of 100 *jembes* per man. Thus the annual production of hoes may be 63,000. Demand for the smiths' products generally exceeds supply. A *jembe* made by a local smith lasts three years, as opposed to five for an industrially produced one (Mothander 1989), but costs half as much. Given the life of these hoes, perhaps 189,000 people are being supplied with *jembes* by the traditional smiths every three years, or 12.3 per cent of the population. No figures exist for the number of people who share a *jembe* within a family unit, but the figures suggest that the traditional blacksmiths are meeting a significant proportion of the demand for hoes in these two regions since they are producing one *jembe* per approximately 8 people every three years. The increase in population since 1988 is likely to be balanced by the number of unrecorded blacksmiths, so 12.3 per cent of the total population remains a reasonable guess. The official planning figure (Tanzania 1992) for hoe demand in Mtwara region for 1990–91 was 270,478 (= 17 per cent of the population, which, as an industrial *jembe* lasts 5 years, is equal to 88 per cent of the population being supplied). However, in the event only 2421 were recorded as being sold to farmers, which is less than 1 per cent of the population over 5 years. It is therefore reasonable to suppose that the bulk of the difference is being met by the traditional blacksmiths.

There are two aspects to this project, skills training and access to scrap steel. Scrap steel is available in the regions from sisal and other agricultural estates, but transport is a major constraint. This is being addressed by providing credit facilities for blacksmiths to purchase cycles and cycle trailers, following careful trials. A cycle trailer can comfortably carry 100kg of steel, enough to make 67 *jembes*. The potential profit from the use of cycle trailers to carry steel is over Tsh40,000 per month, depending on distance and road conditions. A cycle and trailer currently costs Tsh80,000, the national minimum wage is Tsh5000 per month. The response from the blacksmiths being trained were uniformly positive, and more than 14 loan applications have been received [since May 1992], applications being rationed because of the under-estimating of the demand upon the credit provision.

While the traditional blacksmiths are currently producing agricultural tools, they lack good tools and do not know how to harden and temper carbon steel correctly. Joseph Marihwi, a blacksmith on ITDG's staff in Zimbabwe, came to Lindi and spent five weeks training six instructors. Two of these were the project staff who had carried out the census, Messrs Maguta and Kitambi, each of whom had selected for training the two most promising traditional smiths from the region which they had surveyed. Of these four traditional smiths the best two were offered positions as trainers at the end of the course, Mssrs Nchela and Mtama. With the ex-ception of files and hacksaw blades, all the tools used on the instructors' courses were made by Mr Marihwi beforehand. During the five weeks of instructor training enough tools were produced to train twenty people at one time in the subsequent training programme.

The four instructors are now working as two training teams, one in each region. Using a motor cycle, a bicycle and two trailers each team carries 120kg of tools to the village where the next training course is to take place. There is a six-week training cycle within which there is a three week train-ing course. Between six and ten smiths are trained on each course, though the pressure of enthusiasm has occasionally pushed numbers as high as 15. Six weeks before a course is due to start the training team leader approaches the appro-priate number of blacksmiths living close together and offers the training course, which is not a rigid syllabus but can be tailored to each group's requirements. The blacksmiths are required to make preparations for the course, preparing charcoal, making bricks and providing an appropriate shel-ter. If these preparations have not been made when the trainers arrive the course will not take place. The course, using the tools made by the instructors, takes three weeks and includes business training as well as the making of chisels, punches, drifts, hammers, hot sets, tongs, tinsnips, drills, screw drivers and spanners and associated techniques such as hardening and tempering. No tools or equipment are given away but each trainee makes their own set of tools during the course, which they keep. No allowances or other fees are paid to the trainees. The SIDO regional economist is supposed to visit the smiths during the course to arrange credit for cycles and trailers for those who wish to acquire them, and also to carry out a subsequent monitoring exercise. The training teams are largely responsible for organizing their own activities, but report to their respective SIDO Regional Managers. The training cycle period also allows for clearing up, monitoring the smiths trained three months before, and a one-week rest period.

The first pair of decentralized courses started on 13th April 1992. During 1992 a total of 107 blacksmiths received the training in their own forges. Because of serious constraints upon the RIPS programme there was minimal supervision of the teams during 1993, but nonetheless 90 blacksmiths were trained during the dry seson at a cost of TSh34,000 (US$69) each; this output will be the norm in future. With one change of trainer in the teams the training is continuing in 1994. The principal shortcomings of the programme have been SIDO's failure to supervise, and the ineffectiveness of their credit programme in relation to cycles and trailers. In 1994 an experiment will be carried out using a traditional system of material supply with the aim of making the training courses self-financing. If this is successful it will be extended to enable the blacksmiths to purchase transport and other equipment by paying in kind.

If the 107 blacksmiths trained during 1992 each serve 100 families averaging five members, the improved quality and range of products and the increased productivity would have benefited approximately 53,500 people in the first year alone. (Since a *jembe* lasts about three years this assumes a very pessimistic average production of less than fifty *jembes* per year, considerably less than one month's production for a reasonable smith with access to material.) In 1993 the cost per person for each of the 45,000 beneficiaries of the training would be TSh68, US 14 cents, of Finnish taxpayers' money. If the introduction of the *nusu-nusu* self-financing system in 1994 proves a success the cost of running each course should reduce to zero. There is considerable interest at SIDO headquarters in the possibility of copying this system in other regions of Tanzania.

The Spoon Foundry of Limete, Kinshasa, Zaire
Four young men live by means of selling the cooking spoons which they cast from scrap aluminium. With the support of

Jack Sier, the Roman Catholic priest who runs the Oxfam programme in Kinshasa, the workshop had been established at an appropriate level. The furnace for melting the aluminium is a truck wheel hub buried in the sand, the air supply coming from a common version of a hand-driven fan. The fuel is hardwood charcoal, the raw material scrap aluminium. The only unduplicatable item of equipment is a cast-iron two-spoon mould imported by Oxfam from Europe, but although this means that the workshop cannot be imitated by others the nature and quality of the mould means that it is likely to last an extremely long time. The shop is in the open air, behind palm frond screens, outside the house of two of the young men. The spoons are sold for 5 zaires each, about five pence at 1986 exchange rates, direct from the workshop, the demand is so great. If conditions are favourable and there is sufficient raw material the four men can cast up to 700 spoons per day, which allows their income to be about five times what they would earn in a factory (in the unlikely event that such a job were available). Unfortunately the supply of scrap metal fluctuates, since an increasing number of small foundries has been set up to cast cooking pots, so their productivity and income are now restricted, but even with only one day's production per week they are still as well-off as they would be working full-time in a factory (were they able to do so).

This workshop was established at a minimal level in terms of both technology and capital, and remains sustainable for this reason. The young men are in control of the business, having received technical support and limited original financial help from Jack Sier. The support given by Oxfam concerned the needs of the consumers and considered the options open to the operators, particularly their need for sustainable employment. The goods the foundry produces are in strong demand from the local population, who cannot afford the industrially produced spoons that are sometimes available in the city. The direct Oxfam involvement was brief, leaving a productive workshop likely to continue to produce useful goods.

Metalwork in Zimbabwe
A frequently heard suggestion is that the development of rural manufacturing enterprises requires the introduction of new products. Since this idea originates generally with

external experts, the identification of new products tends to be led by their own ideas of what might sell.

Possessing specialist capacity in metalworking, ITDG wished to examine ways in which this might be employed to assist the rural poor in Zimbabwe, in common with their other programmes. A survey was conducted of the relevant rural areas to establish the goods currently available (and those needed but unavailable) and to identify the sources of supply. By comparing these findings with the manufacturing resources of the rural areas it was possible to ascertain where the shortcomings in supply lay, both in terms of availability and quality. Detailed analysis of consumer preferences was of particular significance, since these were based on an intimate knowledge of the employment of the articles in question.

Once the needs of the target group, the rural poor, and the existing capability of the artisans had been established, particular areas where some support to the artisans would increase their ability to serve their communities were identified. As a by-product, the individual craftsmen would also benefit, since their prosperity is vital in encouraging the support activity; it is important, however, that such benefits are not the primary aim, as this lessens the emphasis on overall rural development, whereby the greatest number of people benefit, and is also likely to put the artisan in a weaker position because the thrust of her or his business is less likely to be appropriate which therefore makes it harder to sustain (Cromwell 1989).

This carefully focused study forms the basis of interventions in partnership with local institutions which share the same goals, and which are concerned that the subject communities should retain control of their own development. The resulting work by ITDG is concentrating upon the development of the instructional base and the training methodology of a number of organizations. The approach is centred upon training craftsmen in an environment similar to that in which they do or will practice, and on decentralization, as is generally being proposed in this book. After one year the project was beginning to produce clear results confirming the validity of the methodology and the contribution it would make to the communities in which the blacksmiths work (ITDG No9 1990). The adoption of the same approach on another blacksmith-training project, in Malawi, has produced a significant improvement in the results from the earlier, less sympathetic approach (ITDG No6 1990).

Fish hooks in Uganda

A Euro-Action Acord project to support rural inland fisher-men in Uganda resulted in a simple but effective development which places one aspect of the means of production firmly in the hands of the local communities. Fish hooks were rarely available in Uganda since they were all externally produced, requiring unavailable foreign currency to import them. The Acord project worker, Derek Wright, working with the local blacksmiths, introduced the making of hooks by entirely artisanal methods, using the simplest of jigs and tools which can be made by the smiths. A subtler virtue of such skill acquisition was demonstrated when Derek noticed that the fish-hook makers were fashioning their tools rather smaller than the ones they had been shown originally. On being asked the reason why one maker patted his pocket, into which all the tools now fitted, and explained that when the security of the area next broke down he would be off over the border into Zaire, his fish-hook factory in his pocket, his means of survival secure.

The matter of respect for religious beliefs and traditions has already been discussed in relation to fire-welding in Manie; Derek's experience and actions echo those conclusions. He became aware that the blacksmiths were reluctant to work in front of him, particularly where the setting up of a new forge was involved. Suspecting that the existence of traditional religious observances was inhibiting them, Derek unobtrusively laid a coin and some bones under the hearth of the forge. Being questioned about this, he explained the traditional practice of British blacksmiths. This led naturally to a discussion of similar local practices, permitting an expression of respect for them and thus a mutual acceptance and dialogue. A partnership which allows the local participants control, and the knowledge that they have it, is not possible without confidence on their part that all of the elements of which their culture and practices consist are recognized and respected, whether disclosed or not (Wright 1988).

External agents

Since virtually all development initiatives involve external agents, usually as the instigators, the way in which they approach their work is significant and has frequently been inappropriate. While the points made in this section can be widely demonstrated in Africa they are inevitably generalizations, and it should be stressed that the exceptions which demonstrate the value of a more perceptive and respectful approach do exist, though they remain very much in the minority.

The nature of externally led change promotes the tendency for the leadership to be directive, and to use a set of priorities which relate to external values. Not only does this lead to inappropriate change, but it does nothing to enhance the capacity of the community to initiate and lead its own development, so creating and reinforcing dependency. However, where development is a collaborative dialogue it can be directed within the community, according to the community's social system and checks, prioritized according to need. The community's ability and willingness to initiate and direct its own development is thereby enhanced, making it increasingly reluctant to be directed or manipulated by outsiders.

The basis upon which external agents usually consider themselves qualified encourages the denigration of existing indigenous knowledge since they are conditioned by their Northern orientation, and are qualified in their own eyes by their academic training and the professional experience based upon it. Knowledge which is not considered to be qualified in a similar way is not given equal respect. In contrast to this, if agents were to start from a position which recognizes the accuracy of indigenous knowledge the resulting respect for it and its possessors would promote its dominance in the development initiatives in which they are involved. Since the qualification of such knowledge is diametrically opposite to that of the agents' it can then be recognized that the usefulness of the Northern-oriented knowledge and experience resides in its ability to support and extend the indigenous knowledge, rather than to supplant it.

In a similar way, most external inputs concerned with enterprise development are designed according to Northern conventions, failing to recognize local social and economic conditions and requirements. For example, Northern-oriented agents tend to assume that the rural economy is integrated totally with the cash economy, even with the formal economy, and to ignore any unquantifiable social relationships and exchanges which may form part of a rural

100

trading relationship. The result is that either the social fabric is impinged upon by their actions or the entrepreneurial input is only partly relevant, making sustainable development unlikely. Agents frequently miss the significance of local consumer needs and preferences, which are directed by the environment in which they occur and therefore possess a high degree of appropriateness to that environment. Again, where credit is made available to small-scale rural entrepreneurs, the system is chosen and directed by the external agents, often without relating it to the cultural context, rather than making it a mechanism which permits the subjects of credit to control its use and so to change the pattern of paternalistic donor control and subservient dependence.

Northern-oriented agents are conditioned to achieve tangible results and are encouraged to do so by project-related funding structures. Since agents' contracts frequently have a short time-scale and contain a specific intention, the tendency is to attempt to change the conditions to favour the planned end result, often by introducing artificial supports and the means of sustaining change in the short term. Where an agent allows her or himself to be an active part of the development initiative, and introduces resources only available through her or him, rather than being a catalyst, sustainability is unlikely because of the dependence this creates. Such inappropriate actions relate to the target rather than the community, whereas with internally directed development the limited experience of the community controls the rate of change and the components within it, making each step more appropriate to existing conditions and experience, and therefore more likely to be sustainable.

The two most significant external inputs intended to promote rural industrialization are credit and training. The use of alien training systems which are not culturally, technically or economically relevant is a major problem, though their inappropriateness generally goes unrecognized. Such systems, originating in industrial societies have been developed for the purpose of supporting large-scale formal-sector industry and its attendant bureaucracy. When people being trained by systems relating to Northern conditions are unlikely to be employed under compatible conditions the training is inappropriate to their needs. In Africa all small-scale rural manufacturing is essentially pre-industrial, in the Northern sense.

In order to be appropriate the content and context of training must relate as closely as possible to the subsequent professional practice of the trainee. As well as course content, the type of workshop accommodation used and the way in which it is equipped, the location of training can also be inappropriate. Northern centralized training systems remove future practitioners from the context in which they will work and do nothing to build up the self-regenerating training capacity of the community itself. Any specialized formal training location will inevitably possess or acquire more sophisticated equipment than the trainee will be likely to require or be able to afford, even with credit, and this is partly due to the perception of training efficiency held by the institution. Not only does this create expectations and dissatisfaction with the trainees' immediate prospects, but it also leads to misconceptions regarding the function and value of capital equipment. Even where the intention is that graduating trainees will work in a rural context such inappropriate training leads them towards the urban formal sector instead.

Unlike centralized formal training, contextual training allows for the continuing development of skills by both direct transfer and empirical development, and facilitates the acquisition of vocational skills by illustrating continually the relevance of the content, and encouraging trainees to judge the validity of what is being transferred, particularly where the training capacity of the community itself has been developed.

Clients and targets

There are two separate but overlapping reasons for assisting the development of rural manufacturing: to give the rural poor access to non-agricultural income-generating opportunities; and to give rural consumers access to the goods and services which they require, something of particular importance where these goods will be used for productive purposes, for example agriculture. Both contribute to the development of rural areas.

In both cases the rural poor usually constitute the target group whom the intervention is intended to assist. In the case of interventions concerned directly with income generation this group is also the client group, being those to whom input is made.

102

Where the purpose is the provision of goods or services to support the rural poor and their activities, the client group may not be the rural poor themselves, but whoever produces or will be able to produce the required goods or services. For example, an intervention concerned with rural blacksmithing in Zimbabwe is concerned primarily with the provision of goods and repair services to the rural poor. In order to improve this provision a project was initiated to develop the capacity and abilities of the rural smiths, the client group, by which means their service to their communities would be improved, to the benefit of the consumers, the target group (ITDG 1989). Such a distinction is significant, since it focuses the purpose of the intervention and makes it more likely that it will be achieved.

One of the indicators by which the successful development of the artisanal client group may be measured is their increased income resulting from their improved capability. If a client artisanal micro-enterprise is to be able to serve its community it must be economically viable, so one of the aims of an intervention will be to place the craftsman in a good position to generate income. However, the purpose of this is to ensure the provision of goods to the community, rather than to improve the financial position of the artisan, which is an incidental benefit. Where the two separate purposes are not understood the agents may consider direct income generation as being the sole reason for the action (ITDG 1988). Considering the artisans as their target group the agents may consult carefully over the direction of the intervention, but the result, giving income-generating opportunities to the artisans, may not benefit the rural poor, who might have been the target group in a clearer analysis.

The involvement which arises from working with any particular group or class tends to emphasize the problems of that group and therefore to make their solution an objective. An agency working with one client group with the intention of benefiting a separate target group will always find it difficult to be objective.

This risk of misdirection becomes greater where the target and client groups are distinct, and where the client group is being influenced at one remove, for example through input to a training institution. In this case the needs of the artisans and the needs and interests of the institution combine to obscure the best interests of the intended beneficiaries. The widespread assistance which is given to training institutions easily becomes inappropriate and even counter-productive.

Just as the appropriateness of an intervention is in inverse proportion to the distance between the control and the target group, the same is true of the distance between the target group and the point at which the intervention is made. If external agents work with centralized institutions, well removed from the target group, there are many opportunities for inappropriate directions to be taken. If the input is made as close as possible in the chain to the point of impact, the target group, the room for misdirection is minimized, while the opportunities for target-group influence over direction are increased. The closer to the target group, the greater the relevance of all participants' contributions.

Success indicators

The most direct indicator of success in the development of rural manufacturing is the survival of a new enterprise, the strengthening of a particular activity which was previously marginal, or the sustaining of productive change.

If a rural producer is able successfully to sustain her or his activity it means that the output is being sold, and therefore has sufficient usefulness to the community to justify the cost and provide an income for the producer. In the case of the blacksmiths of Manie in Zaire, for example, the continued manufacture of the new products introduced by the author, demonstrates the demand for them and therefore their relevance (Poston 1988). When the choice of input and the selection of products have been made by the practitioners the chances of the development being maintained are far higher than when they lack the control. Although they might be prepared to undertake initial experiments to please the external agent, blacksmiths would not continue to make a product for which there was no demand. By the same token, customers in a penurious village do not buy products for which they have no need, so continued production indicates that the community has benefited from the input. A simple indicator is the successful generation of additional income. For example the significantly increased income enjoyed by the blacksmith Mr Mazambani of Dedza in Malawi arose directly from the training which he had received and the subsequent use which he had made of it (ITDG 1988).

Where the products are primarily useful for other productive purposes, as is particularly the case with blacksmithing, the widespread use of locally produced tools is an indicator of their value and the contribution made by their producers to the local economy. Following the successful introduction of the Manie smiths to the making of hammer heads, correctly hardened and tempered chisels, plane blades and other tools, the immediate demand for these products by consumers and the interest from other practitioners in acquiring the new skills indicated success in meeting a local need and in exploiting a market opportunity (to the financial benefit of the smiths) (Poston 1989). The UNDP/ILO blacksmithing project near Dhaka in Bangladesh is a good example of a project where the primary purpose and therefore also the main indicator was the improvement of the smiths' income, though other producers benefited, through improved access to tools. Hand-made tools are successfully selling both locally and to the urban formal-sector market in competition with imported industrially made Chinese tools, the price of which they are undercutting by over 50 per cent. In this case technical and marketing improvements were reinforced by the introduction through credit facilities of grinding machines which permitted a great improvement in the quality of finish given to the tools (Uddin 1989).

As in the case of the Bangladesh blacksmiths, a discernable improvement in the quality of the product is measurable, and has several benefits, including increased suitability for function, increased artisan confidence, greater competitiveness with industrially produced items and an increased income for the maker. This results in less outflow of cash from the village, a possible net cash gain and sometimes even a saving of foreign exchange.

If a development initiative is truly successful and has become an established part of local practice requiring no further support or participation from the external agent, certain other qualities relevant to the sustenance of the activity will be evident. Skills will be developed beyond those which originally existed and those which have been transferred, showing that the activity has acquired its own dynamism. As part of this process some product development may be looked for, both in terms of existing process or product improvement and of the introduction of new products by the artisans themselves. Evidence of such innovation is a crucial

105

indicator of the potential of the activity to prosper and develop, since it can only do so if it is not confined by the *status quo* of the practitioners' existing capacity. A prerequisite for innovation is confidence, since it involves the risk of failure. With successful innovation and subsequent consumer response comes a level of pride in the maker's ability. If an initiative is to be considered successful there must be no dependence upon any external agent or artificially sustained condition; self-confidence, pride and the ability to use the existing capacity as a basis for innovation indicate this state.

Where markets and raw materials are accessible, the dynamic independence described above will demonstrate itself through the duplication of the activity, either through the training and subsequent release of apprentices, or through imitators. While imitation may result in a faster spread of the activity, apprenticeship will bring about a surer dissemination of the skills involved, and therefore of the requisite quality. Imitation without training does carry a risk of a degradation of the skills and of product quality, which is eventually likely to damage all those involved. An indicator of success, therefore, is not only the extent to which the capacity has spread, but the degree to which quality has been maintained through this process. Where it has been possible to develop a self-sustaining mechanism to maintain the quality of any duplication, the long-term health of the activity will be more assured.

An ultimate indicator of success is the subsequent autonomous development of local systems concerned with particular aspects of the activity. Such systems might include group action to improve access to raw materials, credit or markets, the growth of subcontracting or the development of some form of professional association. At Manie, for example, the group of smiths evolved into the Comité du Cadre, concerned with the further development of the group and the improvement of standards and trading relationships. Such actions demonstrate the changed manner in which the practitioners have come to view themselves and the possibility of affecting their own situation. This change in their attitude also manifests itself through a healthier relationship with external agents, who come to be regarded as supportive colleagues or associates with whom issues are discussed, as opposed to donors on whom the responsibility for change is seen to rest. A further indicator of the changes in the self-image of the participants and the manner in which they conduct themselves and their business is the manner in which they have come to be regarded by people outside their immediate activity, particularly those in authority or controlling resources.

While some indicators are more precise than others, and the occurrence of them will depend upon the circumstances and degree of success, it should be stressed that all are interrelated. Excessive reliance should not be placed solely upon quantifiable factors, since these can be misleading. Fundamental success is demonstrated by the growth in self-esteem resulting from the growth of capability.

5. The way forward

The manner of interventions

THE EASY ASSUMPTION BY external agents of the responsibility for making an intervention is a matter for grave concern, since in many cases the comparative ability of the agent and the client to be making appropriate decisions lies clearly in favour of the client. Since, however, the resources and therefore the control lie with the agent, who is unlikely to recognize her or his lack of qualification, the client is likely to remain marginalized. Interventions which follow this pattern create minimal benefits, particularly in the long term, and are likely to have negative effects. If the role of the agent is that of a conduit for the needs, wishes and intentions of the target group the responsibility is not assumed in the same way, but remains as far as possible with those who will benefit or suffer from the effects of any consequent change. The key players must be the target group, not the external agents, and any intervention must be justified solely in terms of the needs of that group.

The results of any intervention need to have two key characteristics, sustainability and duplicability. The need for sustainability is obvious, since a beneficial development which does not endure is a waste of everybody's effort, time and money, and will be a negative experience for those whom it was intended to benefit. In the case of entrepreneurial activities profit is a necessary component of sustainability, since without it the business will fail. Romantic or doctrinaire attitudes imposed upon the realities of a commercial activity in a marginal economy are an indulgence on the part of those concerned and will not contribute to the continuation of the enterprise. Sustainability is even more frequently undermined by the selection of inappropriate components for an enterprise which are either financially unsound or which cannot be sustained without continued external support.

The problems facing rural Africa and the scale on which

they exist make projects which affect only small groups quite inadequate. Since a depressingly high number of interventions have no lasting benefit, the need to maximize the impact of those which are beneficial is extremely urgent. As has been discussed earlier, large-scale interventions are generally inappropriate, particularly in the context of small and micro enterprise. In order to have a significant impact any intervention should be specifically designed for duplication without the need for additional external input.

Given the significance of the activity of part-time blacksmiths in rural Africa, if the consolidation of each workshop requires individual external support they will remain marginalized, in spite of their growing relevance in a changing economic environment. If such workshops require some input in order to survive, let alone to improve their service to the community, but if individual attention is impractical, then this vital resource will be lost unless the mass of workshops can be affected without being contacted directly by external agents. The concept of entrepreneurial 'packages' created by external agents is not sufficient, since by their nature each package is likely to require individual installation and support.

Where an intervention and its component parts are entirely appropriate the potential exists for autonomous propagation, the input being adopted and spread by practitioners and would-be entrepreneurs without any further reference to outside influence, to an extent where the original input may be judged to have had a significant effect in relation to the scale of the problem. The carrying out of interventions which have this specific goal in mind has the great virtue that the input is immediately subject to choice, editing and adaptation by those who will use it and be included among its beneficiaries. If the original intervention was inappropriate it will not propagate in this manner, limiting automatically any damage it might otherwise do if it were artificially spread by continued external support. A good example of such propagation exists in many of the projects which have been developed and promoted fuel-efficient cooking stoves such as the *jiko* stove in Kenya. Following seminal work by ITDG and other organizations these stoves are now the province of the commercial sector, enjoying huge success because of their economical performance and the associated improvement of the domestic environment. It is worth pointing out that the styling and working of the stove relate closely to the far less efficient stoves that were previously in local use; the changes were kept within the limits of what people were accustomed to, and were therefore more readily acceptable.

Unless an intervention has clearly defined objectives which can be fully justified, and corresponds with the needs of the target group, it is likely to be unfocused, ineffective and potentially harmful. Every component must be examined carefully to check that it does indeed serve the objectives. It is easy for the immediate strategy to dominate and redirect an intervention, particularly where the outlook of those making an input leads to an obscuring of the objectives.

In a paper-making project run by a missionary organization near Feni in Bangladesh, which was intended to generate income for destitute women, the concern of the external agents to produce desirable products gradually dominated the decision-making process. The choice of capital equipment was influenced primarily by the product quality which would result rather than by the employment created, where a poorer but more labour-intensive product might still have been saleable and have met the income-generating objective more fully. In the same way processes were subcontracted to urban commercial firms for the manufacturing of more sophisticated products where the externally added value was far greater than the value of the paper material made by the women. Rather than analysing what skills the women would acquire and what processes could be carried out in-house and then designing around them, knowing what the threshold of quality was in the marketplace, the agents had become excessively concerned with the quality of the products which could be produced, for their own sake. If the objective of the project was to generate as much income as possible, every production decision should have been taken with that as the only yardstick. While a few employment opportunities were lost by the installation of powered pulping equipment the more serious impact was that the whole operation could not be duplicated by those requiring an income at this level; if a group of women left the project after a couple of years it would not be possible for them to reproduce the activity viably.

The target group of an intervention is those whom it is intended to benefit. This group, and how it is to benefit, should be clearly defined. The client group is those with whom the intervention will be made, in order to achieve the objective. These two groups are not always made up of the same people, as has been discussed earlier. Confusion between the two is likely to produce results which were not intended and may negatively affect the relationship between them when their identity does not coincide. On other occasions the client group themselves constitute part of the target group. An example of this is in an ITDG project concerning Bangladesh where the principal target group is the rural poor consumers served by the blacksmiths (the client group) who, being landless poor themselves and large in number, also constitute a target group for whom the objective is income generation (ITDG 1990).

If any development is to be sustainable it must be based upon a thorough understanding of the context in which it will occur if inappropriate inputs were to be avoided. Respecting the knowledge of both target and client groups, and working with them as closely as possible in order that their knowledge guides the intervention and maximizes its appropriateness is essential. The previous norm within donor-dominated projects was to rate the expertise of the expatriate highly and to give less credence even to equivalently qualified nationals, while local people without formal qualifications were dismissed largely as having almost nothing of significance to offer. As has been discussed earlier, such judgements arise out of the prejudice of those in control who value their own form of knowledge most highly and are frequently incapable of recognizing the validity of different forms, particularly when these are unmeasured. The example from Malawi of the regulation whereby a qualified technical instructor with no blacksmithing experience had to be recruited to work with traditional smiths in spite of the existence of unqualified but more suitable practitioners exemplifies this (ITDG 1988).

It is desirable therefore, that project staff should be nationals wherever possible, and they should be chosen for the relevance of their knowledge and their ability to communicate with the target group. Additional training can be given if there are specific deficiencies. In activities such as blacksmithing this means that project staff should include traditional blacksmiths in preference to formally trained instructors as was the case in the SIDO project in southeastern Tanzania. The experience and understanding of an

111

instructor used to teaching young men in a technical institution may be a disadvantage when working with mature practising skilled smiths. Institutional attitudes can also be inappropriate in this context. On an ITDG-organized training course for Malawian institutional instructors at the Glen Forest Training Centre, Harare in 1989, one training instructor objected strongly to eating the same food as ordinary trainees at the centre in their company, since he felt this to be demeaning (ITDG 1989). Such an attitude of superiority is totally irreconcilable with a respect for the existing knowledge of those with whom one is working.

While subconscious prejudices may lead those controlling interventions to feel confidence in formal qualifications, a goal should be the use and development of existing practitioners to carry out any direct training work. For example, an intelligent and skilled practising traditional blacksmith can be taught new technical and didactic skills. His experience makes his perceptions extremely valuable, and he will be able to communicate with the client group on an equal and unequivocal footing. The training of such a local instructor has the additional benefits of developing a training capacity which it may be possible subsequently to retain within the community and of validating the knowledge of all the local smiths rather than denigrating it by importing the resource.

Since the aim in this case would be to train practising rural smiths, one of their number should be able fully to absorb all that it is necessary for them to be taught, and how to teach it. If it is felt that a more knowledgeable or skilled instructor is needed it is likely that the knowledge which it is intended to transfer is excessive and inappropriate. Discussing business training for micro-entrepreneurs, Mark Havers of the Durham University Business School pointed out that if one needed three different specialists for the purpose then obviously too much was being taught for one entrepreneur to absorb. One instructor should be able to convey the knowledge which must be retained and used by an entrepreneur carrying out all the business functions himself (Havers 1990). Extending this argument, it should be possible for one instructor to transfer all the different technical and entrepreneurial skills and knowledge required by a self-employed artisan; if it is not, then clearly too much is being required of the artisan on the receiving end. When the blacksmiths of Manie decided to pass on what they had learned to other smiths within their area they were very effective, imitating the instructional methods with which they had themselves been taught. Although they enjoyed the prestige, the gaining of which encouraged them to share their knowledge, their social relationships did not permit them to patronize their peers.

Interventions concerned with the development of manufacturing enterprises, whether for their own sake or for the benefit of a third party, should be guided by careful research in both the markets for the goods and the artisans' access to those markets. Whether the target group is the artisans or the consumers, it is the existence and scale of the market which determines the success of an intervention. Even if markets do exist they are of no use to the artisans if they cannot get reliable and independent access to them.

A project run in Bangladesh by the Bangladesh Small and Cottage Industries Corporation and the International Labour Organisation (Uddin 1990) helped highly skilled rural blacksmiths to develop alternative products, such as Northern-style carpentry tools with a ground finish. There proved to be a limited market for these tools which were of a pattern not normally used in the country and for which the principal market is urban; in addition, the limited working capital of the smiths meant that they had difficulty reaching these urban markets and were very much at the mercy of local merchants, who bargained accordingly. Appropriate market and market access research would have allowed the project better to fulfil its objectives.

Opportunities which exist for the penetration of markets outside the community offer the benefit of inward cashflow and should be exploited. However if a local demand for the skills exists this should be given priority, since the direct support of the rural community is most important. Assisting the development of access to services for the community and to income for the artisans is more useful than only the latter, unless there is a particular need for the community to have varied sources of cash income. Where the local economy is vulnerable to natural disasters, such as floods or droughts which can destroy the agricultural basis of the community's economy, a source of income which is independent of agriculture and the consumers of the local community whom it supports offers some protection against destitution. An example of this is the more than 150 women who sell poor quality pottery to tourists on the Beitbridge Road south of

Masvingo in Zimbabwe. Though they make few sales and little money it is a totally different source of income from their land, which receives sufficient rainfall for a crop only every three or four years. The pottery justifies the considerable effort necessary for such small returns.

Important in understanding the market is a knowledge of acceptable and desirable quality in comparison to price. There is invariably considerable knowledge regarding these factors among target and client groups, as well as among remote consumers who are not target or client, which should be tapped. This applies also to the processes of manufacture. Normally the closer that any transferred technique lies to existing local practice and skills the higher the quality of the product will be, since this minimizes the proportion of new skill required. The opinions and perceptions of both producers and consumers regarding process analysis and selection offer a valuable guide to the most appropriate process, even when a new product requiring unfamiliar techniques is being considered.

All technical interventions should make the local technical *status quo* their starting point and then work to find the means by which the product can be made with the least input and change. The majority of external agents approach interventions with an image of the point, familiar to them, which they wish the artisans to arrive at. The two are not normally compatible. Added to the other arguments against traumatic change from the familiar to the transferred is the risk that the recipients of a transfer which is significantly alien may subsequently perceive technology as something which can come only from outside the community. Enterprise development which reinforces attitudes of dependency is self-defeating.

This author is convinced that the first priority for intervention is to work with existing artisans in order to consolidate their base of appropriate skills, on which subsequent rural manufacturing development depend. This does not preclude the training of initiates, for whom the appropriateness of inputs is quite as important as it is for their practitioner elders.

Approach to training

The majority of skills training in Africa is carried out in technical institutions modelled upon their Northern equivalents and is concerned principally with Northern qualifications.

Blantyre Polytechnic in Malawi, for example, has a significant complement of British lecturers carrying out their tasks in the same way that they would in the UK. The Northern pattern of technical education is designed to provide appropriately trained labour for modern industry, which it does moderately well, and fulfils the same purpose in Africa to a certain extent. But the general application of this type of training fails to recognize that for many trainees it is inappropriate, particularly where they will pursue artisanal trades. Most craftsmen in Africa will work in the informal sector, both rural and urban. The rural context is a pre-industrial one for which industrially oriented training is of minimal use. For example, Mudikosi of Vanga, Zaire spent three years learning metalwork at the Institut Technique de Kikwit, two years being concerned entirely with machine tools. There was subsequently no work for him unless he migrated to Kinshasa, where prospects would be very uncertain, so he chose to retrain as a blacksmith under the tutelage of the traditional smiths at Manie. Not only are many of the curricula inappropriate but even when the subject matter could be of vocational use the equipment of the institution is normally of a type which any trainee going to work in the informal sector is never likely to see again. Many graduates have considerable problems adjusting to this extreme difference in resources.

This now even applies to hand tools. In many institutions graduates would once have been presented with a tool kit, but for financial reasons this is now an almost universal impossibility. Aaron Moore's work with ITDG has successfully introduced the making of their own tools to many carpentry students, but is hampered by students' perception that wooden carpentry tools are second-rate, since students were trained originally on imported steel tools. Where institutions understand the significance of these factors and alter their policy concerning workshop equipment the benefits are considerable. At Silveira House, an independent training centre near Harare, the woodworking and blacksmithing instructors are now adamant in their refusal to have any purchased tools among the equipment, since they believe that it would undermine the appropriate self-sufficiency to which their trainees become accustomed.

Any intervention concerned with artisanal training for rural manufacturing is likely to recruit formally qualified instructors who will come conditioned by their training and understandably proud of their professional knowledge. Faced with the needs of practising or would-be rural artisans they will apply to the problem that which they have learned in their institutions, perpetuating the inappropriateness of input and guaranteeing the inefficacy of the intervention, to the detriment of those whom it was intended to benefit. The decisions which lead to this situation are made by others trained by Northern standards whose judgement has been similarly misdirected. Frequently there is donor influence from expatriates who are not only qualified in the North but whose experience in an industrial society has convinced them of the value of their training and knowledge, allowing them to insist upon the virtue of their conventional wisdom.

If adherence to Northern training systems is inappropriate for both practitioners and future instructors, the training in the North of technical instructors and decision-makers is even more inappropriate and unhelpful. Northern institutions have a limited knowledge of the conditions to which their African graduates will return, and are likely to reinforce the credibility of Northern solutions. The expectations raised by such a period of study also encourage ambitions which can only be met by finding more elevated employment than working as an artisanal instructor. There are certain professional areas and levels for which foreign study becomes desirable, but for those who are being trained as artisanal instructors it is inappropriate and distracting. If the necessary training resource only exists outside the country it is better to use the funds to develop it in-country as a local resource from which far larger numbers can benefit, rather than for counterproductive foreign study for the few. Where training is impossible within the same country the use of a compatible context elsewhere within the region is preferable to training in the North.

Within any intervention there should be not only the immediate objective but also the intention to support and build the local capacity to achieve such objectives without expatriate assistance. It is important that local institutions should be fully involved in all interventions, assisted by any external agents who may be necessary (or whose presence is an obligatory condition made by the funders). However, since many training institutions may adhere to the pattern outlined above, it should not be assumed automatically that they are the most suitable collaborators on interventions concerned with the sustenance of rural manufacturing. The possibility of working with institutions which are closest to the need or the client group rather than with institutions who appear to fulfil the right function must be considered. The work done with the smiths of Manie was facilitated and supported by the Lusekele Agricultural Centre which had never previously concerned itself with artisans, but recognized their significance to the Centre's target group. This concern with the objective, without prejudice about the best manner in which it might be reached, allowed the intervention to develop naturally under the direction of the blacksmiths themselves.

The further training is removed from the context in which it will subsequently be applied the greater is the risk of acting upon mistaken assumptions, and the more likely it is that unrealistic expectations will be raised. If an instructor works with a group of trainees under a tree or a thatch similar to the workshops which they can aspire to he is less likely to introduce equipment or techniques which are inappropriate. If the same instructor is equipping a centralized training workshop he will install whatever convenience equipment he can, which he will then teach the trainees to use. If the employment outlook for a trainee is as a village craftsman with minimal equipment, training him in a conventionally equipped workshop with basic power tools places him at a disadvantage when he tries to work under his tree without those facilities. A frequently heard argument against in-context training is that it is logistically too difficult to carry all the equipment necessary into the field. This is true if a conventional training workshop is to be transported. However if the in-context training is to be appropriate there will be a minimal amount of equipment. Each trainee village should be taught to make as much of her/his own equipment as possible if future access is to be assured. All that is therefore required initially is the most basic set of tools with which each trainee can create the workshop equipment and tools with which they will subsequently be able to start their professional life. In order that the trainees' confidence in the tools they make should not be undermined it is essential that the tools with which the training course is initiated should be identical to those which they will learn to make.

Just as the introduction of any development must be self-sustaining if it is to have a significant effect, so the support of

117

rural manufacturing requires the development of an appropriate training capacity as close to the location of need as possible. If training is centralized it will be remote from the needs to which it relates, the training skills not belonging to or under the control of the communities which they should serve. Since some degree of grouping of training resources is inevitable, care should be taken that such centres are kept as close to their clients as possible — certainly being located in rural areas — and that the various tiers of training structure reach right down to the village level. Dependency upon remote institutions, particularly foreign ones, weakens the community's ability to develop itself.

It is highly desirable that trainers at all levels remain in close touch with the communities they serve by spending time working there rather than paying the occasional formal visit. The work for which people are being trained is dirty-handed; it is important therefore that the instructors are seen to be dirty-handed also. A considerable barrier to adopting this approach is the lack of motivation of many instructors. The products of formal education, with expectations to match, these instructors need a clearer understanding of what constitutes fitness for purpose in a trainer.

Traditional artisan training, both in Africa and the North, is by apprenticeship. Among the advantages of this system are the perpetuation of specialized local knowledge, the development of relevant practical skills, the ability to solve problems in relation to their context and social appropriateness; the apprentice becomes fully integrated with her or his context. Among the disadvantages are the difficulty with which developments of knowledge or skill will enter the system and the restriction of knowledge within social groupings. A training system exploiting the virtues of the traditional while improving access to knowledge originating externally would therefore be appropriate.

Extension training is well-established in the agricultural context in various forms, and is equally relevant to rural manufacturing. In the case of artisans occasional visits by a peripatetic extension agent are not likely to prove sufficient. A more appropriate means is to make inputs to a number of selected and motivated practitioners who are identified locally as the masters. Extension input and specific training is then provided to these masters who in turn support and train locally practitioners in an extended form of informal apprenticeship. This constitutes the establishment of a local training capacity and has the advantage that, although new knowledge is entering the community, most basic training will be done by locals rather than by external agents. In this way the ground covered and the number of people affected by the peripatetic trainers is far greater than for a similar amount of money spent on centralized training, even allowing for payment to the masters, should this be desirable. In addition, the closer to the practitioner level that training skills are developed, the more likely they are to remain within the community. The initiation of the concept of the Centre Technique de la Forge Traditionelle at Manie was based upon this approach.

The practising or intended rural artisans are the consumers of the training, so it is logical that all inputs should be tailored accurately to their needs in both nature and manner of delivery. In addition to the need for technical training there is a need for knowledge in related areas, particularly entrepreneurial. However, the enthusiasm of specialists in particular subjects tends to inflate the amount and type of information considered necessary for the practitioner. It must never be forgotten that all the knowledge necessary to manufacture products and conduct the enterprise will be the responsibility of just one person, the artisan. One way of restricting the overload which training may attempt to place upon the practitioner is to use only one instructor for all training inputs relating to the enterprise. If one instructor is not able to retain all the relevant information, the artisan trainee will certainly not be able to.

To assist the absorption of appropriate entrepreneurial knowledge and to ensure its relevance to subsequent practice the teaching of it should be integrated with the technical subject to which it relates. In this way when a piece of raw material is picked up in the workshop its value is automatically mentioned and seen as an integral part of its recognition. Time spent on work should also be recognized, so that at the end of any manufacturing training exercise there exists both an artefact and an awareness of its cost and commercial value. If (minimal) records also kept during the training period, and the tangible products of the training are marketed as an integral part of the exercise, then all the necessary inputs can be covered as an organic whole. This approach has been used successfully in Zimbabwe and

119

Malawi by ITDG in the training of both rural practitioners and instructors. Among other measures, the curriculum of the short courses run by ITDG's local partners includes a couple of 'production days' whose results are measured. Different practices and products are quantified and compared, the results of the two days, one at the start and one near the end of the course, being compared. Additional working in the evenings or at week-ends is also encouraged, and the proceeds of the trainees' industry belongs to the them.

Autonomous propagation requires knowledge and the means by which it can be communicated independently, without recourse to unsustainable artificial external assistance. Autonomous propagation must be the object of all training and training systems if significant development of rural manufacturing industry is to occur.

Implications for intervention agents

Development is a process of gradual growth, as opposed to the introduction of sudden change. Where specific targets exist, progress towards them should be incremental, evolving from small changes. However, because the majority of interventions and projects is concerned with a specified end result the design of the intervention is worked back from that point, so achieving the target inevitably dominates the thinking of the external agents. The process by which the target is reached is therefore given less importance, and is likely to suffer from pragmatic action taken to promote the achievement of the target. This tendency is exacerbated by the common use of short-term contracts, particularly for managerial and specialist expatriates, whose cultural conditioning is that of tangible achievement and whose future careers depend upon measurable successes achieved within limited time-frames. Short-term contracts not only affect the approach of the staff concerned, but, where project duration is longer, cause considerable disruption through change-overs and the consequent re-evaluations and re-ordering of priorities. It is significant that, among expatriates, missionaries are much more likely to be involved in long-term evolutionary development work than their Northern NGO colleagues, since their time horizon is far longer and there is not usually the same career pressure. They also have a greater opportunity to understand the needs and priorities of those with whom they are working.

If rural manufacturing is to develop in a sustainable manner the time-frame of interventions must be longer than the short projects and contracts which are currently the norm, so that the process of development can be given the care and attention that is necessary if any target achievement is to be sustained in the long term.

Because donor control and influence is powerful among the partner NGOs who are the intermediaries of a great deal of financial aid, the target orientation of the North is frequently imposed within and through them. In many cases expatriate advisors dominate and emasculate the local director, driving forward for short-term achievement. While local staff are also likely to be conditioned to achieve by their Northern-style education they are at least likely to be involved for a longer period, though the frequent professional musical chairs due to shortage of skilled personnel and political shifts commonly negate this advantage. Expatriates whose professional experience, cultural conditioning and need to achieve leads them to be directive within a development context are counter-productive, since the results of their influence are not sustainable. Intervention agents should avoid the directive attitudes which characterise the North's patronizing contribution to development, and should avoid placing expatriate personnel in positions where they will be able to undermine sustainability.

Within projects the use of artificial components which cannot be sustained socially or commercially must be avoided at all costs, since unsustainable external support within commercial mechanisms distorts the results and leads to the collapse of the system when the support is withdrawn. The avoidance of non-sustainable inputs is likely to frustrate those who measure success over the project period rather than waiting for at least five years after the end of the project, but will lead to far less frustration on the part of the subjects of the interventions.

Access to credit is frequently presented as a major constraint upon the development of small enterprises, including rural manufacturing. While the unavailability of cash resources, particularly for working capital, is a barely surmountable problem for many artisans, the careless provision of credit can be every bit as damaging as the lack of it. Where excessive loans are made available the economic balance of an enterprise can be threatened and the capacity of the artisan to manage resources exceeded. In addition to this, conditioned attitudes of dependency can promote non-repayment and the diversion of funds, exacerbated by the pressures of the extended family. The availability of credit is essential to the development of rural manufacturing, but its scale must be strictly in proportion to the enterprise concerned and its ability to sustain the loan. Loans must be only a component within a more complete support scheme, ensuring that technical, entrepreneurial and marketing skills are also sufficient for the purpose for which the loan is given. The provision of credit must be sympathetic and careful, serving the purpose of development without being a non-commercial and therefore non-duplicatable intervention. Carelessness and a lack of attention to the context on the part of the provider of credit risks the destruction of the enterprise.

Since existing practices and practitioners exist within the contextual *status quo*, they also define it. It is therefore essential that the nature of and reasons for the practices are well-understood by any external agent. This understanding must extend to the social, technical, environmental and economic constraints which have determined the limits to the growth of the activity. A clear recognition of the resources, pressures and constraints encourages respect for the practitioner and her or his capabilities, which forms a sound basis for future collaboration leading to sustainable growth. Compared to the external agent the practitioner is in an incredibly weak and vulnerable position, and is painfully aware of the fact. The basis of any partnership is respect; without partnership there will be no sustainable development. It is therefore vital that the external agent respects the practitioners, and shows it clearly, in order that the external agent approaches existing practices with respect and in a spirit of learning, since the practices are often in balance with the other components of the enterprise. An example of this was an early blacksmithing pilot project supported by ITDG in which the problem of soft-wood charcoal requiring more air in order to burn sufficiently hot for forging was responded to by the development of an inappropriate turbine forge fan which was never subsequently imitated, because of capital cost and complexity. It then took two years to prove clearly that a well-constructed pair of traditional goat-skin bellows was quite sufficient for the task, and the engineered design could be discarded. (ITDG, NO6 1988).

A lack of respect indicates a conviction on the part of the external agent that she or he possesses knowledge superior to that of the practitioner. Being an assumption, this will lead to errors of judgement which the agent is in a position to impose. These errors are most likely to involve the agent's perception of what is appropriate.

Given that an artisan's ability to innovate is fundamental to the survival of a rural manufacturing enterprise, and that innovation requires risk-taking, the development of the confidence of practitioners is fundamental to any attempt to develop their activity. Self-respect is most easily damaged by a lack of respect on the part of others. The simplest and most basic attitude of the external agent therefore enables or undermines the potential for sustainable benefit from the whole intervention.

The clear establishment of what practice or hardware is or is not appropriate in a particular situation would appear to be straightforward, but is rarely achieved. There are many ways in which input or suggested practices may be inappropriate, involving cultural, social, gender, environmental or other factors, but the most frequent error lies in the relationship between the capital cost of an input and the income-generating potential of the market for which it will be producing. If the cost of capital equipment is disproportionate to the income which it will generate, the business will not be sustainable and, if credit is involved, is likely to saddle the entrepreneur with unredeemable debts. Since the markets accessible to rural manufacturers are normally rural themselves and therefore extremely limited in cash terms, their ability to support the capital investments of enterprises is correspondingly limited.

External agents whose short-term goals are to create business start-ups frequently start from a product idea. While the product might be useful and desirable to the market, if it is not within the means of sufficient people (or of a high-enough priority) its production will not be viable. While this is obvious, encouragement to enter production which is not market-led is commonplace.

In order to counter the entrepreneurs' recognition of economic reality capital investment is often heavily subsidized or even provided free. While this enables the external agent to score by creating or developing an enterprise the achievement is limited, since it cannot be duplicated without similar subsidy. It is not uncommon in such cases that the business turnover is insufficient to meet the costs of consumables or maintenance, should spares even be available, resulting in the subsequent abandonment of the equipment in question.

Even more frequent are attempts to improve the quality of an existing product through the introduction of improved capital equipment or the use of additional techniques and artisan time. Although the practitioner and his or her customers are likely to be fully aware of the virtue of the improvement it is often the case that the resources of the customer do not permit the option of buying the better quality item, because of its higher cost. Practitioners are left either to continue to manufacture at the lower quality which customers can afford or improve their quality but continuing to sell at the lower price. The latter option subsidizes the customers' access to better quality, but has the compensation that the better quality goods will sell more quickly than the lower quality competition. Practitioners who are in a position to vary the quality of their output according to market demand sometimes do so, improving product quality as the competition increases. This is particularly evident among the better tinsmiths around Harare. The departure point for the assessment of the economic appropriateness of a product or process is the market demand and purchasing power.

Whether or not entrepreneurs are in a better position than external agents to judge what is appropriate it is important that they should be allowed and encouraged to make the decisions, since the making of comparative choices, Analytical Decision Making, is an essential entrepreneurial ability. External agents should minimize the number of choices which they make on the entrepreneurs behalf, since decisions involve risk and it is the entrepreneur who will be taking the risk. Where technical input is involved it is highly desirable that the presentation of a single possibility is avoided, since this gives the practitioner no choice of appropriateness. One design of equipment or a single method of process suggests that, backed by the authority of the external agent, this is the only way in which the thing can be done. By contrast, if several options are presented to the artisan with the appropriate back-up information, she or he will be in a position to make an informed choice which will minimize the risk of an inappropriate solution based on false assumptions being imposed by the agent. This approach encourages an understanding of the fact that there is no single way to reach a desired end and that technical solutions can therefore be adapted or developed locally by the practitioners themselves.

There are innumerable examples of the 'good ideas' of external agents which, being introduced, have turned out to be disasters for those they were intended to assist. It is easy to ascribe such failures to the inadequacy of the agents concerned and to continue in the belief that one's own projects are sound, based on reason and target group input rather than inspired assumption. 'Good ideas' are easy to identify in others but difficult to recognize when they are your own, so accurate base-line studies and subsequent careful broad-reaching monitoring are essential in every case. Although this is expensive it is cheaper than continually repeating the same errors, and is some small protection for the intended beneficiaries. In most projects the monitoring ceases with a final evaluation at the end of the active project period. If monitoring is to have real value, showing whether interventions have truly worked, it is important that subsequent follow-up assessment be carried out, perhaps two and five years after the active project has ended. Africa is full of the shadows of development projects which were counted as successes when the agents departed at their completion.

If development interventions are to have any value their effect must be indefinitely sustainable. Since the problems which interventions are designed to meet recur so frequently, a development which is individually sustainable but which cannot be duplicated is insignificant. If the duplication of a development depends upon the provision of the same inputs by an external agent each time, the change which can be achieved is also insignificant in the face of the scale of the problems. If significant change is to result from an intervention the development itself must become the agent for change. It must be sustainable and, more than being duplicateable, it must be capable, once established, of autonomous propagation. If the development is not sufficiently appropriate and beneficial, to the extent that people will take it up for themselves, it is unlikely to prove significant in the long term. If the change is too sudden, too expensive or inappropriate in other ways people will not adopt it even for the time required to test it, and it will fail. All the parts of an intervention should be designed from the start with the purpose of enabling and encouraging autonomous propagation.

To permit sustainability and autonomous propagation rural manufacturing developments must be incremental, must not demand great change or significant risk on the part of the practitioners, and must involve a cost low enough to make them widely accessible and viable.

Bibliography

Andrews, Jack (1991) *Edge of the Anvil: a Resource Book for the Blacksmith*, IT Publications.

Anon (1988) 'Education Without Jobs', *African Concord*, 7 June.

Archer, L. Bruce (1974) *Design Awareness and Planned Creativity in Industry*, Design Council.

AT Development Association (1977) *Appropriate Technology – Directory of Machines, Tools, Plants, Equipments, Processes and Industries*, Vol. 1, AT Development Association.

Austen, Ralph (1987) *African Economic History*, James Currey.

Azad, Gulab Singh (1988) 'Development of entrepreneurship among rural women – an overview, *Small Enterprises Development, Management and Extension Journal*, XV, June.

Ballard, R.A. (1979) *Metals for Engineering Craftsmen*, CoSIRA.

Ballyn, John (1986) Producer Assistance Manager, Oxfam Trading, Bicester, UK, interview 8 May.

Baranson, Jack, (1967) *Technology for Undeveloped Areas*, Pergammon Press.

Barker, C.E. *et al.* (1986) *African Industrialisation*, Gower Publishing.

Baynes, Ken (1976) *About Design*, Design Council.

Bealer, Alex W. (1984) *The Art of Blacksmithing*, Harper and Row (3rd ed. revised and updated by Charles McRaven).

Berg, Nimpuno, van Zwanenberg (1978) *Towards Village Industry, A Strategy for Development*, IT Publications.

Betz, M.J., McGowan, P., Wigand, R.D. (1984) *Appropriate Technology: Choice and Development*, Duke Press Policy Studies, Durham, North Carolina.

Bodgaert, Michael, in Carr, M. (1985) 'Adult education and development'.

Borremans, Valentina (1979) *Guide to Convivial Tools*, R.R. Bowker Co.

Boye, David (1977) *Step-by-Step Knifemaking – You Can Do It*, Rodale Press.

Bradley, Ian (1978) *Metalworking Tools and Their Uses*, Model and Allied Publications.

Bradley, Ian (1971) *The Amateur's Workshop*, Model and Allied Publications.

Brammer, Hugh (1980) 'Some innovations don't wait for experts: a report on applied research by Bangladeshi peasants', *Ceres*, March–April.

Brand, Stewart, Ed. (1980) *The Next Whole Earth Catalogue – Access to Tools*, Random House.

Brokensha, David, Warren, D.M., Werner, O. (1980) *Indigenous Knowledge Systems and Development*, University Press of America, London.

Bruno, Brother, Driefontein Mission, Mvuma, Zimbabwe, (1989) interview.

Butcher, Donald, B. (1989) 'The development of business or the business of development?' unpublished paper, Institution of Civil Engineers.

Callaghy, Thomas M., 'The political economy of African debt: the case of Zaire' in Ravenhill, 1986: 314, 331, 342.

Campbell, Alastair *et al.* (1977) *Worker-Owners: The Mondragon Achievement*, Anglo-German Foundation for the Study of Industrial Society.

Carr, M. (1982) *Appropriate Technology and Rural Industrialisation*, IT Pubs.

Carr, M. (1976) *Economically Appropriate Technologies for Developing Countries*, IT Publications (revised 1981).

Carr, M. (1985) *The AT Reader*, IT Publications.

Carruthers Ian (1985) *Tools for Agriculture: A Buyer's Guide to Appropriate Equipment*, IT Publications.

Center for Business Information (1980) *AT Organisations – A World-Wide Directory*, McFarland.

Chambers, Robert (1983) *Rural Development: Putting the Last First*, Longman.

Charnock, Anne (1985) 'Appropriate technology goes to market', *New Scientist,*, 9 May.

Cluley, Robin (1987) 'Tool production in Kenya and Zimbabwe: report on a field trip March–April 1987', unpublished, Tools For Self Reliance.

Congdon, R.I. (1977) *Introduction to Appropriate Technology*, Rodale Press.

Council for Small Industries in Rural Areas *The Blacksmiths Pattern Book*, (CoSIRA is now the Rural Development Commission).

Crighton, Peter. Rural Development Advisor Oxfam, Kananga, Zaire, interview (14.9.86).

Cromwell, G.J. and Harries, D.V. (1989) 'Production, repair and use of metal goods in rural Zimbabwe', ITDG, unpublished.

Dawson, Jonathan (1988) 'Small-scale industrial development in Kumasi, Ghana', unpublished paper, Brunel University.

Fall, A., Ndiame, F., Djibelor, C. (1988) 'La Traction Animale pour le Développement Agricole', paper, West African Animal Traction Network.

Fernando, S. and Gamage, W. (1989) 'Some oscio-political aspects of Janasaviya', unpublished paper, IRED, Colombo.

Frensman, N. (1982) *Industry and Accumulation in Africa*, Heinemann.

Gamanga, E.B. (nd) 'Traditional education of blacksmithery among the Mendes of Sierra Leone', unpublished, Institute of Adult and Extra-mural Studies, Fourah Bay College, University of Sierra Leone.

Gamser, Matthew S. (1988) 'Power from the people — technology users and the management of energy innovation', *Energy Policy*, February.

Gamser, Matthew S. (1988) 'Innovation, technical assistance, and development: the importance of technology users, *World Development*, Vol. 16, No. 6: 711–21.

Ghosh, Pradip K. (ed) (1984) *Appropriate Technology in Third World Development*, Greenwood Press.

Gibson, Dutch, interview at IRDP Mpika, Zambia 1986.

Gibson, Dutch, (1980) 'Build your own metal-working shop from scrap: designing and building the sheet metal brake, Vol. 7', Gingery.

Gibson, Dutch, (1980) 'Build your own metal-working shop from scrap: the charcoal foundry, Vol. 1, Gingery.

Gibson, Dutch, (1980) 'Build your own metal-working shop from scrap: the drill press, Vol. 5', Gingery.

Gibson, Dutch, (1981) 'Build your own metal-working shop from scrap: the metal shaper, Vol. 3', Gingery.

Gibson, Dutch, (1981) 'Build your own metal-working shop from scrap: the milling machine, Vol. 4', Gingery.

Gibson, Dutch, (1982) 'Build your own metal-working shop from scrap: the dividing head and deluxe accessories, Vol. 6', Gingery.

Gibson, Dutch, (1982) 'Build your own metal-working shop from scrap: the metal lathe, Vol. 2', Gingery.

Haaland, Randi and Shinnie, Peter (1985) *African Iron Working — Ancient and Traditional*, Norwegian University Press.

Hammond, Ross W. (1976) 'Employment generation through the stimulation of small-scale-industry', Nos 1, and 3), Georgia Institute of Technology.

Haque, M.M. and Islam, M.N. (1990) 'Promoting indigenous innovations: the case of blacksmithy in Bangladesh', paper published in *Tinker Tiller*, IT Publications.

Harper, J.D. (1981) *Small-scale Foundries for Developing Countries*, IT Publications.

Harper, Malcolm (1984) *Small Business in the Third World*, John Wiley.

Harper, Malcolm and Soon, T.T. (1979) *Small Enterprises in Developing Countries — Case Studies and Conclusions*, IT Publications.

Harries, David (1987) 'Metalworking in Sierra Leone (and Ghana)', unpublished, VSO.

Harries, David, in Cromwell, G.J. and Harries, D.V. (1989) 'Production, repair and use of metal goods in rural Zimbabwe', ITDG, unpublished.

Harrison, Paul (1979) 'Small is appropriate', *New Scientist* UK, 5 April.

Havers, Mark (1990) Durham Business School, seminar on Small Enterprise Development at ITDG.

Helmsing, A. (1987) 'Non-agricultural enterprise in the communal lands of Zimbabwe', University of Zimbabwe Occasional Paper Vol. 10, Harare.

Higgott, Richard (1986) 'Africa and the new International division of labour' in Ravenhill 1986.

Hitchings, Rob (1985) *How to Make a Folding Machine for Sheet Metal Work*, IT Publications.

Hitchings, Rob and Tanburn J. (1985) 'Tour report of Malawi and Botswana', unpublished, ITDG.

Hojbak, A. (1980) 'Establishment of small-scale rural workshops (for light engineering goods) in East Africa' in UNIDO (1980).

Holtermann, Sally (1979) *Intermediate technology in Ghana: the experience of Kumasi University's Technology Consultancy Centre*, IT Pubs.

Hommel, Rudolph P. (1969) *China at Work*, MIT Press.

Hopkins, A.G. (1973) *An Economic History of West Africa*, Longman.

Hosier Richard H. (1987) The informal sector in Kenya: spatial variation and development alternatives', *Journal of Developing Areas*, No. 21, July.

Hounkonnou, D. (1988) 'Stemming the rural exodus: city opportunities in the villages', *The Courier* No. 107, Jan–Feb.

Howes, Michael and Chambers, Robert (1989) 'Indigenous technical knowledge: analysis, implications and issues', in Brokensha, 1980, p. 326.

Hulscher, Wim and Fraenkel, Peter (1993) *The Power Guide: An International Catalogue of Small-scale Energy Equipment*, IT Publications.

Hultcrantz, Gerhard (1978) 'The development of small-scale industry in Mwanza Region' in Berg, L., *et al. Towards Village Industry*, IT Publications.

Hussey, Simon (1989) Organization of Rural Associations for Progress, Bulawayo, Zimbabwe, interview.

India, Government of (1985) *Economic Survey 1984–85*, Lloyds Bank Group Economic Report.

ITDG (1988) project reports NO6B04, unpublished.

ITDG (1988–90) NO6B04/A04 project files, unpublished.

ITDG (1989) NO8B01 project reports, unpublished.

ITDG (1990) NO9B02, unpublished project files.

ITDG (1990) N10B01, unpublished project files.

Inversin, Allen R. (1980) 'How to build a blacksmith's bellows', *Appropriate Technology*, Vol. 6 Part 4, pp.7–9.

Jacob, Frère (1986) Institut Technique Professional de Kikwit, Bandundu, Zaire, interview 3 December.

Jéquier, Nicholas (1976) *Appropriate Technology: Problems and Promises*, OECD.

Jéquier, Nicholas (1979) *Appropriate Technology Directory*, OECD (Development Centre).

Jonsson, Lars Ove (1986). (Swedish International Development Agency), Chief Agricultural Engineer, Rural Structures and Equipment, Ministry of Agriculture and Water Development, Lusaka, Zambia, interview, 4 November.

Kahn, J.S. (1980) *Minangkabau Social Formations — Indonesian Peasants and the World Economy*, Cambridge University Press.

Katakwe, Antonio (1986) interview Lusaka, Zambia, 7 January.

Kencare, A.S. (1975) 'Technology for the developing world', CME.

Kenya, Republic of (1979) Development Plan, 1979–83, in Carr, M., *The AT Reader*, IT Publications.

Khurana, I.R. (1988) 'Whither rural industrialisation?' *Yojana* (India), May 1–15.

Kienbaum Report, in Muller, Jens (1980) *The liquidation or consolidation of indigenous technology*, Aalborg University Press.

Kitching, Gavin (1982) *Development and Underdevelopment in Historical Perspective*, Methuen.

Kiyenze, B.K.S. (1985) 'Jipemeyo — the transformation of Tanzanian handicrafts into co-operatives and rural small-scale industrialization,' Finnish Anthropological Society.

Klein, Bernat (1976) *Design Matters*, Secker and Warburg.

Kohr, Leopold (1980) 'The breakdown of nations', in Sale, 1980, p. 82.

Kropotkin, Peter (1974) *Fields, Farms and Workshops Tomorrow*, ed. Colin Ward, Allen & Unwin (1st ed. 1899).

Kumar, Satish (ed.) (1980) *The Schumacher Lectures*, Blond and Briggs.

Lamont, Victor, Director, 'Global Village', South Petherton, Somerset, UK, interview 24 March 86.

Langdon, Steven (1986) 'Industrial dependence and export manufacturing in Kenya', in Ravenshill (p. 181 and pp. 181–211).

Langdon, Steven and Mytelka, L. 'Africa in the changing world economy', in Legum *et al.* (p. 170).

Larsson, Gustav, Ohlsson, Lennart, Tembo, Gaban, and Jacobson, Ellen (1985) 'Study on Katapola Agricultural Engineering Centre in Eastern Province and a review on vocational technology units at IRDP Northern Province and IRDP Luapula Province: a preliminary report', unpublished, Ministry of Agriculture and Water Development, Zambia.

Laye, Camara (1954) *The African Child*, Fontana Books.

Liedholm, C. and Mead, D. (1987) 'Small-Scale Industries in Developing Countries: Empirical Evidence and Policy Implications, Michigan State University.

Lipton, Michael (1977) *Why Poor People Stay Poor: Urban Bias in World Development*, Temple Smith, London.

Little, I.M.D. (1989) 'Small manufacturing enterprises and employment in developing countries', source unknown, (via ODA Library service, D189–0070).

Livingstone, Ian 'Alternative approaches to small industry promotion', in Frensman, 1982.

Livingstone University College, Dar es Salaam, 'The National Small Industries Corporation of Tanzania: an examination of current plans and prospects', in Berg, 1978.

Lloyds Bank Group (1985) *India: Economic Report*, Lloyds Bank, London, p. 17.

Lützen, Jacob, KR Jeweller Ltd, Lusaka, Zambia, interview 7 November 86.

Macpherson, G.A. (1975) *First Steps in Village Mechanisation*, Tanzanian Publishing House, Dar Es Salaam.

Malama, Mr, Malama Brothers, Mpika, Zambia, interview 13 November 86.

Mann, R.D. (1972) *How to Make a Metal-Bending Machine*, IT Publications.

Marks, Vic (ed.) (1977) *Cloudburst: a Handbook of Rural Skills and Technology*, Cloudburst Press.

Marsden, Keith (1970) 'International labour review', in Carr, M., 1985.

Marshall, Ken (1983) *Package Deals — a Study of Technology Innovation and Transfer*, IT Publications.

Mason, L.C. (1977) *Building a Small Lathe*, Model and Allied Publishers, Argus Books.

Mayall, W.H. (1979) *Principles in Design*, Design Council.

McRobie, George (1981) *Small is Possible*, Jonathon Cape.

Melanesian Council of Churches (ed.) (1977) *Liklik Buk*, Liklik Buk Information Centre (PO Box 1920, Lae, PNG).

Miles, D.W.J. (1982) *Appropriate Technology for Rural Development: the ITDG Experience*, ITDG.

Minto, S.D. and Westley, S.B. (1975) *Low Cost Rural Equipment Suitable for Manufacture in E. Africa*, E. African Agriculture and Forestry Research Organisation.

Mitchell, R.J. (1980) *Experiences in Appropriate Technology*, Canadian Hunger Foundation.

Moeran, Brian (1984) *Lost Innocence. Folk Craft Potters of Onta, Japan*, University of California Press.

Moore, Aaron (1986) *How to Make Twelve Woodworking Tools*, IT Publications, London.

Moore, Aaron (1987) *How to Make Planes, Cramps and Vices*, IT Publications, London.

Moore, G. (1979) 'New shoots from old roots', *Development Forum*, August/September.

Mothander, B., Kjaerby, F., Havnevik, K. (1989) *Farm Implements for Small-scale Farmers in Tanzania*, Scandinavian Institute for African Studies, Uppsala.

Mountjoy, Alan B. (1975) *Industrialization and Developing Countries*, Hutchinson.

Moyes, Adrian (1979) *The Poor Man's Wisdom: Technology for the Very Poor*, Oxfam, Oxford.

Mudikosi, metalworker interviewed at Vanga, Bandundu, Zaire, 22 February 88.

Mulenga, Mr, Mesco Products Ltd, Kitwe, Zambia, interview 21 November 86.

Muller, Jens (1980) *The Liquidation or Consolidation of Indigenous Technology*, Aalborg University Press.

Nalumansi, S.R. (1988) 'Initial survey related to rural industrialisation of Niger State'. Unpublished paper, Development Technology Unit, Warwick University.

Neck, Philip and Nelson, Robert (1987) *Small Enterprise Development: Policies and Programmes*, International Labour Organisation.

Nelson, George (1979) *Design*, Architectural Press.

Ngulube, Mr, Acting General Manager of Small-scale Enterprise Promotions Ltd, Development Bank of Zambia, Lusaka, Zambia, interview, 10 November 86.

Nilsson, Torre (nd) *Where to Find New Products to Manufacture*, Torre Nilsson Publications, Hamburg.

North, Richard (1986) *The Real Cost*, Chatto and Windus, London, (p. 52).

Oliver, Peter, Zambia Consolidated Copper Mines, Lusaka, interview, November 1986.

Omae, Kim (1985) 'Canadian Patent Office: a little-used information resource', *Canadian Commerce*, March.

Papanek, Victor (1972) *Design for the Real World*, Thames and Hudson.

Paris, P. and Hutin, S. (1985) *Promotion de la Petite Industrie*, Groupe de Recherche et d'Échanges Technologiques (GRET).

Pilditch, James (1976) *Talk About Design*, Barrie and Jenkins.

Pilger, John (1986) *Heroes*, Jonathan Cape, London.

Pirie, John (1986) Director, Oxfam Trading, Bicester, UK, interview 9 April 86.

Point (1974) *Whole Earth Epilog — Access to Tools*, Penguin.

Poston, David (1985) 'A survey of equipment in metalworking workshops', Humberside College of Higher Education, Hull, unpublished.

Poston, David (1987) 'A tool-making project with the blacksmiths of Manie, Zaire', unpublished.

Poston, David (1988) 'The dissemination of technical knowledge among the blacksmiths of Bandundu Region, Zaire, unpublished.

133

Poston, David (1988) 'Metalworking in Luapula Province, Zambia', report for the Provincial Planning Unit, Mansa, Luapula, unpublished.

Pye, David (1968/78) *The Nature and Art of Workmanship*, Cambridge University Press.

Pye, David (1983) *The Nature and Aesthetics of Design*, Herbert Press.

Rao, C.H.N. and Mohan, C.U. (1988) 'Grass-root entrepreneurship and rural industrialisation'. *Small Enterprises Development, Management and Extension Journal*, Vol. XV, No. 1 March.

Rao, Radhakrishna (1983) 'Earthscan bulletin', in Carr, M., 1985.

Rau, Koka Kesava (1975) Report on Agricultural Implements and Machinery Production and Maintenance, FAO/UNIDO project URT/74/006/A/OL/12, Dar es Salaam.

Ravenhill, John (1986) *Africa in Economic Crisis*, The Macmillan Press, London.

Riedijk, W. (ed.) (1982) *Appropriate Technology for Developing Countries*, Delft University Press.

Roy, D.P. (1988) 'Industrial policy and development of rural industries in Bangladesh: a review of some issues', *Industry and Development* No. 24, UNIDO.

Rybczynski, Witold (1980) *Paper Heroes*, Prism Press.

Sale, Kirkpatrick (1980) *Human Scale*, Coward, McCann and Geoghegan, New York.

Sandesara, J.C. (1988) 'Small-scale industrialisation: the India experience'. *Economic and Political Weekly*, 26 March.

Schirra, Gerd (1986) (Friedrich Ebert Stiftung) Small-scale Enterprise Promotions Ltd, Development Bank of Zambia, Lusaka, Zambia, interview, 10 November.

Schmitz, Hubert (1984) 'Industrialisation strategies in less developed countries: some lessons of historical experience', *Institute of Development Studies*, Vol. 19: 1–21.

Selig, Gary, Director, Centre Agricole de Lusekele (CBZO), Bulungu, Bandundu, Zaire, interviews July 1987 and June 1989.

Serkkola, Ari 'Rural Development in Tanzania: a Bibliography.' Institute of Development Studies, Helsinki University 1987.

Sharman, M. and Prasad, R. (1988) 'Blacksmiths — the technologists of the rural poor', *Moving Technology*, Vol. 3, No. 5 October.

Sier, Jack (1986) Oxfam Kinshasa Project, interview, November.

Sigurdson, Jon (1974) 'The role of small-scale and rural industry and its interaction with agriculture and large-scale industry in China', mimeo, Stockholm School of Economics.

Singer, Hans (1977) *Technologies for Basic Needs*, International Labour Office, Geneva.

Sinha, Sanjay (1983) 'Planning for rural industrialization' (1983), in Carr, M., 1985: 374.

134

Siziba, Mr, Metal Workshop Owner, SIDO Industrial Estate, Mumbwa Rd, Lusaka, Zambia, interview, 6 November 86.

Smillie, Ian (1986) *No Condition Permanent*, IT Pubs.

Staley, E.F. and Morse, R. (1965) *Modern Small Industry for Developing Countries*, McGraw Hill, New York.

Stewart, Frances (1977) 'Technology and Underdevelopment', in Carr, M., 1985: 113.

Sutcliffe, Bob (1984) 'Industry and underdevelopment re-examined', Institute of Development Studies, Vol. 19: 121–33.

Swanson, Richard A. 'Development interventions and self-realization among the Gourma' in Brokensha, 1980: 67–8.

Tanzania, Government of (1969) 'The second five-year plan for economic and social development (1969–1974), Vol. 1: 133, Dar es Salaam.

Tanzania, Government of (1972) *The Economic Survey, 1971–72*, The Government Printer, Dar es Salaam, tables 29 and 30.

Tanzania, Government of (1991) *Statistical Yearbook*, Dar Es Salaam.

Tanzania, Government of (1992) Annual Reports Submitted to the Office of the Prime Minister and First Vice-President, Dar Es Salaam.

Taylor, Gabrielle, OXFAM, interview 12 December 86.

Tchimbangila, Kamanga, 'Institut Technique Professionel', Mbuji-Mayi, Zaire, interview 10 December 86.

Thomas, A. and Lockett, M. (1978) *Choosing Appropriate Technology*, Open University Press.

Thomas, Terry (1985) 'Training for technology choice', unpublished report, ITDG.

Tornatzky, L.G. *et al.* (1983) *The Processes of Technological Innovation: Reviewing the Literature*, National Science Foundation.

Torp, Erling, NORAD Volunteer, Kitwe, Zambia, interview 21 November 86.

Townsend, Robert (1980) *Further Up the Organisation*, Coronet Books.

Traoré Amadou (1981), 'The courier', in Carr, M., 1985.

Tucker, Ted (1980) *Practical Projects for the Blacksmith*, Rodale Press.

Uddin, Jamal Ahmed, Interview re ILO/UNDP project BGD/86/070, Bangladesh March 1990.

United Nations Economic Commission for Africa (1983) 'ECA and African development, 1983–2008', ECA, Addis Ababa.

UNIDO (1974) *Animal Drawn Agricultural Implements, Hand-operated Machines and Simple Power Equipment in the Least Developed and Other Developing Countries*, United Nations Industrial Development Organisation.

UNIDO (1980) 'Appropriate Industrial Technology for Light Industries and Rural Workshops' (Monograph on Appropriate Industrial Technology No. 11) United Nations, New York: 81.

135

UNIDO (1969) *Bicycles: A Case Study of Indian Experience,* United Nations.

UNIDO (1970) *Design, Manufacture and Utilisation of Dies and Jigs in Developing Countries,* United Nations.

Vail, David J. (1975) 'Technology for Ujamaa village development in Tanzania', Maxwell School of Citizenship and Public Affairs, Syracuse University, USA: 8.

Van Dijk, M.B. (1982) 'The technology gap in the case of small enterprises development in Riedijk, W. *Appropriate Technology for Developing Countries,* Delft University Press: 55, 56.

Van der Merwe, N. and Avery, D.H. (1987) 'Science and magic in African technology: traditional iron smelting in Malawi', *Africa* Vol. 57, No. 2.

Van Rensburg, Patrick (1974) 'Report from Swaneng Hill; education and employment in an African country, The Dag Hammarskjöld Foundation: 39, 68.

Vogler, Jon (1983) *Jobs From Junks: How to Create Employment and Tidy Up Derelict Cars,* IT Publications.

Volunteers in Technical Assistance (1975) *The Village Technology Handbook,* VITA.

Von Krogh, Fie, NORAD Volunteer, Kitwe, Zambia, interview 22 November 86.

Wakefield, Rowana and Stafford, Patricia (1977) 'AT, what it is and where it is going', *The Futurist,* April.

Warburton, L. (1980) *Electro Plating for the Amateur,* Model and Allied Publications.

Watkins, M.T. (nd) *Metal Forming I — Forging and Related Processes,* Oxford University Press.

Webber, Ronald (1972) *The Village Blacksmith,* The Country Book Club.

Weygers, Alexander, G. (1978) *'The Recycling, Use and Repair of Tools',* Van Nostrand Reinhold.

Williams, V.C. (1977) 'Rural uplift through village industries', unpublished report, Village Industry Service, Zambia.

World Bank (1987) *World Development Report.*

Wright, Derek (1988) interview, November and, with Pitcher, Kevin, (1988) 'The artisanal production of fishing hooks in developing countries', unpublished.

Zambia, Ministry of Agriculture and Water Development (1980) (Rural Structures and Equipment Dept.), Lusaka, Zambia, 'Rural mechanisation pilot project in Central Province', unpublished paper.

Zambia, Ministry of Agriculture (1978/9) File on rural mechanization pilot project in Central Province, unpublished.